I0450444

Adaptive Harvest Management
2001 Duck Hunting Season

PREFACE

The process of setting waterfowl hunting regulations is conducted annually in the United States. This process involves a number of meetings where the status of waterfowl is reviewed by the agencies responsible for setting hunting regulations. In addition, the U.S. Fish and Wildlife Service (USFWS) publishes proposed regulations in the *Federal Register* to allow public comment. This document is part of a series of reports intended to support development of harvest regulations for the 2001 hunting season. Specifically, this report is intended to provide waterfowl managers and the public with information about the use of adaptive harvest management (AHM) for setting duck-hunting regulations in the United States. This report provides the most current data, analyses, and decision-making protocols. However, adaptive management is a dynamic process, and information presented in this report may differ from previous reports.

Citation:	U.S. Fish and Wildlife Service. 2001. Adaptive Harvest Management: 2001 Hunting Season. U.S. Dept. Interior, Washington, D.C. 47pp.

ACKNOWLEDGMENTS

A working group comprised of technical representatives from the USFWS, the four Flyway Councils, and the U.S. Geological Survey (USGS) (Appendix A) was established in 1992 to review the scientific basis for managing waterfowl harvests. The working group subsequently proposed a framework of adaptive harvest management, which was first implemented in 1995. The USFWS expresses its gratitude to the AHM Working Group and other individuals, organizations, and agencies that have contributed to the development and implementation of AHM. We especially thank D. J. Case and Associates for help with information and education efforts.

This report was prepared by the USFWS Division of Migratory Bird Management. F. A. Johnson (USFWS) was the principal author, but significant contributions to the report were made by J. A. Dubovsky (USFWS), W. L. Kendall (USGS Patuxent Wildlife Research Center), M. T. Moore (USFWS), J. A. Royle (USFWS), and M. C. Runge (USGS Patuxent Wildlife Research Center). D. J. Case (D.J. Case & Assoc.), G. W. Smith (USFWS), and K. A. Wilkins (USFWS) provided information or otherwise assisted with report preparation. Comments regarding this document should be sent to Jon Andrew, Chief, Division of Migratory Bird Management - USFWS, Arlington Square, Room 634, 4401 North Fairfax Drive, Arlington, VA 22203.

Cover art:	Robert Hautman's rendering of a northern pintail (*Anas acuta*), which was selected for the 2001 federal "duck Stamp." (The image has been reversed to function better as cover art for this report).

TABLE OF CONTENTS

Annual reports and other information regarding adaptive harvest management are available online at:
www.migratorybirds.fws.gov/reports/reports.html

EXECUTIVE SUMMARY

In 1995, the USFWS adopted the concept of adaptive resource management for regulating duck harvests in the United States. The adaptive approach explicitly recognizes that the consequences of hunting regulations cannot be predicted with certainty, and provides a framework for making objective decisions in the face of that uncertainty.

The original AHM protocol was based solely on the dynamics of midcontinent mallards, but efforts are being made to account for mallards breeding eastward and westward of the midcontinent region. The ability to regulate harvests on mallards originating from various breeding areas is complicated, however, by the fact that a large degree of mixing occurs during the hunting season. The challenge for managers, then, is to vary hunting regulations among flyways in a manner that recognizes each flyway's unique breeding-ground derivation of mallards. For the 2001 hunting season, the USFWS will continue to consider a regulatory choice for the Atlantic Flyway that depends exclusively on the status of eastern mallards. This arrangement continues to be considered provisional, however, until the management implications of this approach are better understood. The recommended regulatory choice for the western three flyways continues to depend exclusively on the status of midcontinent mallards.

For the 2001 season, the USFWS is maintaining the same regulatory alternatives as those used during 1997-2000. The prediction of harvest rates associated with these regulatory alternatives now must account for the possibility of a regulatory choice in the Atlantic Flyway that is different from other flyways. Analyses suggest that the harvest rates of midcontinent mallards depend almost completely on regulatory choices in the three western flyways. Harvest rates of eastern mallards, however, depend not only on the regulatory choice in the Atlantic Flyway, but on the regulatory choice in the remainder of the country (principally the Mississippi Flyway). We accounted for this dependency in the calculation of an optimal regulatory strategy for the Atlantic Flyway.

Optimal regulatory choices for the 2001 hunting season were calculated using: (1) stock-specific harvest-management objectives; (2) the same regulatory alternatives as in 2000; and (3) four alternative population models and their updated weights for midcontinent mallards, and eight alternative models for eastern mallards, equally weighted. Based on this year's survey results of 8.7 million midcontinent mallards (federal surveys plus state surveys in MN, WI, and MI), 2.7 million ponds in Prairie Canada, and 1.0 million eastern mallards, the optimal regulatory choice for all Flyways is the liberal alternative.

The AHM Working Group continues to pursue a number of priorities in the development of AHM. Foremost among these are efforts to incorporate multiple mallard stocks, as well as other duck species, in the decision-making protocols of AHM. Progress with mallards has been slowed somewhat, however, by the need to review all the data and models for all mallard stocks, and by the need to consider how regulations based on mallards might affect those of other species. Ultimately, the ability to take advantage of variation in stock-specific harvest potentials will be influenced by stock-specific harvest-management objectives (which remain unclear), and by our ability to regulate stock-specific harvests (which is imprecise). Therefore, the AHM Working Group is attempting to better articulate the issues of concern in the future development of AHM, and to provide useful guidance to the USFWS, Flyway Councils, and other stakeholders.

BACKGROUND

The annual process of setting duck-hunting regulations in the United States is based on a system of resource monitoring, data analyses, and rule making (Blohm 1989). Each year, monitoring activities such as aerial surveys and hunter questionnaires provide information on harvest levels, population size, and habitat conditions. Data collected from this monitoring program are analyzed each year, and proposals for duck-hunting regulations are developed by the Flyway Councils, States, and USFWS. After extensive public review, the USFWS announces a regulatory framework within which States can set their hunting seasons.

In 1995, the USFWS adopted the concept of adaptive resource management (Walters 1986) for regulating duck harvests in the United States. The adaptive approach explicitly recognizes that the consequences of hunting regulations cannot be predicted with certainty, and provides a framework for making objective decisions in the face of that uncertainty (Williams and Johnson 1995). Inherent in the adaptive approach is an awareness that management performance can be maximized only if regulatory effects can be predicted reliably. Thus, adaptive management relies on an iterative cycle of monitoring, assessment, and decision making to clarify the relationships among hunting regulations, harvests, and waterfowl abundance.

In regulating waterfowl harvests, managers face four fundamental sources of uncertainty (Nichols et al. 1995, Johnson et al. 1996, Williams et al. 1996):

(1)   environmental variation - the temporal and spatial variation in weather conditions and other key features of waterfowl habitat; an example is the annual change in the number of ponds in the Prairie Pothole Region, where water conditions influence duck reproductive success;

(2)   partial controllability - the ability of managers to control harvest only within limits; the harvest resulting from a particular set of hunting regulations cannot be predicted with certainty because of variation in weather conditions, timing of migration, hunter effort, and other factors;

(3)   partial observability - the ability to estimate key population attributes (e.g., population size, reproductive rate, harvest) only within the precision afforded by existing monitoring programs; and

(4)   structural uncertainty - an incomplete understanding of biological processes; a familiar example is the long-standing debate about whether harvest is additive to other sources of mortality or whether populations compensate for hunting losses through reduced natural mortality. Structural uncertainty increases contentiousness in the decision-making process and decreases the extent to which managers can meet long-term conservation goals.

AHM was developed as a systematic process for dealing objectively with these uncertainties. The key components of AHM (Johnson et al. 1993, Williams and Johnson 1995) include:

(1)   a limited number of regulatory alternatives, which describe Flyway-specific season lengths, bag limits, and framework dates;

(2)   a set of population models describing various hypotheses about the effects of harvest and environmental factors on waterfowl abundance;

(3)   a measure of reliability (probability or "weight") for each population model; and

(4)   a mathematical description of the objective(s) of harvest management (i.e., an "objective function"), by which alternative regulatory strategies can be evaluated.

These components are used in a stochastic optimization procedure to derive a regulatory strategy, which specifies the appropriate regulatory alternative for each possible combination of breeding population size, environmental conditions, and model weights (Johnson et al. 1997). The setting of annual hunting regulations then involves an iterative process:

(1)   each year, an optimal regulatory alternative is identified based on resource and environmental conditions, and on current model weights;

(2)   after the regulatory decision is made, model-specific predictions for subsequent breeding population size are determined;

(3)   when monitoring data become available, model weights are increased to the extent that observations of population size agree with predictions, and decreased to the extent that they disagree; and

(4)   the new model weights are used to start another iteration of the process.

By iteratively updating model weights and optimizing regulatory choices, the process should eventually identify which model is most appropriate to describe the dynamics of the managed population. The process is optimal in the sense that it provides the regulatory choice each year necessary to maximize management performance. It is adaptive in the sense that the harvest strategy "evolves" to account for new knowledge generated by a comparison of predicted and observed population sizes.

MALLARD STOCKS AND FLYWAY MANAGEMENT

Significant numbers of breeding mallards occur from the northern U.S. through Canada and into Alaska. Geographic differences in the reproduction, mortality, and migrations of these mallards suggest that there are corresponding differences in optimal levels of sport harvest. The ability to regulate harvests of mallards originating from various breeding areas is complicated, however, by the fact that a large degree of mixing occurs during the hunting season. The challenge for managers, then, is to vary hunting regulations among Flyways in a manner that recognizes each Flyway's unique breeding-ground derivation of mallards. Of course, no Flyway receives mallards exclusively from one breeding area, and so Flyway-specific harvest strategies ideally must account for multiple breeding stocks that are exposed to a common harvest.

The optimization procedures used in AHM can account for breeding populations of mallards beyond the midcontinent region, and for the manner in which these ducks distribute themselves among the Flyways during the hunting season. A globally optimal approach would allow for Flyway-specific regulatory strategies, which for each Flyway would represent an average of the optimal harvest strategies for each contributing breeding stock, weighted by the relative size of each stock in the fall flight. This "joint optimization" of multiple mallard stocks requires:

(1)   models of population dynamics for all recognized stocks of mallards;

(2)   an objective function that accounts for harvest-management goals for all mallard stocks in the aggregate; and

(3)   modification of the decision rules to allow independent regulatory choices among the Flyways.

Joint optimization of multiple stocks presents many challenges in terms of modeling, parameter estimation, and computation of regulatory strategies. These challenges cannot always be overcome due to limitations in monitoring and assessment programs, and in access to sufficient computing resources. In some cases, it may be possible to impose constraints or assumptions that simplify the problem. Although sub-optimal by design, these constrained regulatory strategies may perform nearly as well as those that are globally optimal, particularly in cases where breeding stocks differ little in their ability to support harvest, where Flyways don't receive significant numbers of birds from more than one breeding stock, or where management outcomes are highly uncertain.

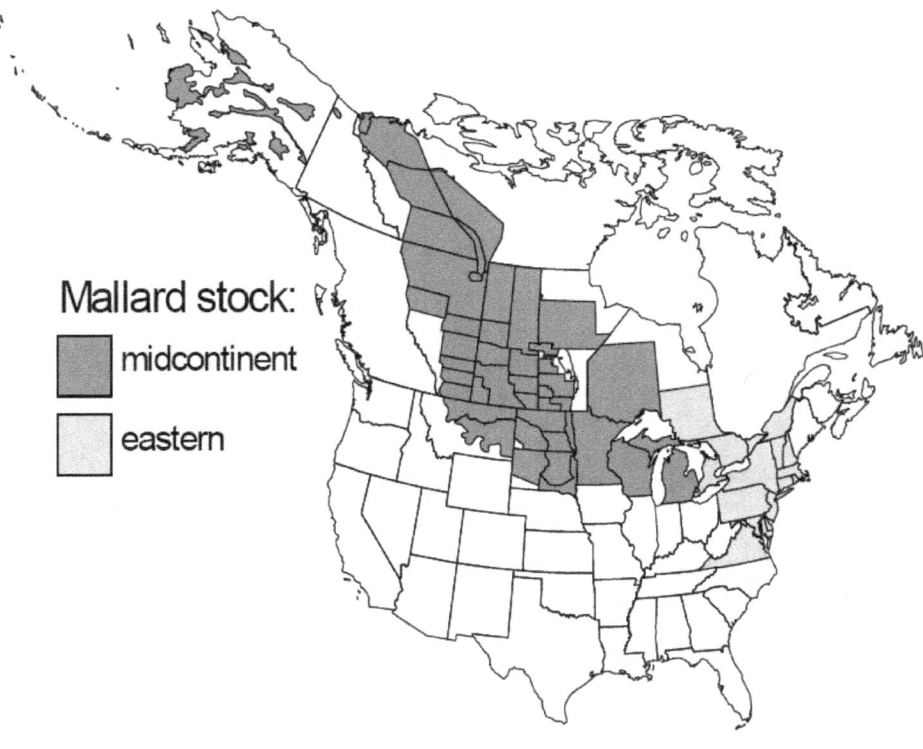

Fig.1. Survey areas currently assigned to the mid-continent and eastern stocks of mallards for the purposes of AHM. Delineation of the western-mallard stock for AHM is pending a review of population monitoring programs.

MALLARD POPULATION DYNAMICS

Midcontinent Mallards

Midcontinent mallards are defined for AHM purposes as those breeding in federal survey strata 1-18, 20-50, and 75-77, and in Minnesota, Wisconsin, and Michigan. Estimates of the entire midcontinent population are available only since 1992 (Table 1).

The dynamics of midcontinent mallards are described by four alternative models, which result from combining two mortality and two reproductive hypotheses. Collectively, the models express uncertainty (or disagreement) about whether harvest is an additive or compensatory form of mortality (Burnham et al. 1984), and whether the reproductive process is weakly or strongly density dependent (i.e., the degree to which reproductive rates decline with increasing population size). The model with additive hunting mortality and weakly density-dependent recruitment (SaRw) leads to the most conservative harvest strategy, whereas the model with compensatory hunting mortality and strongly density-dependent recruitment leads to the most liberal strategy (ScRs). The other two models (SaRs and ScRw) lead to strategies that are intermediate between these extremes.

Table 1. Estimates (N)[a] of midcontinent mallards breeding in the federal survey area (strata 1-18, 20-50, and 75-77) and in the states of Minnesota, Wisconsin, and Michigan.

Year	Federal surveys		State surveys		Total	
	N	SE	N	SE	N	SE
1992	5976.1	241.0	977.9	118.7	6954.0	268.6
1993	5708.3	208.9	863.5	100.5	6571.8	231.8
1994	6980.1	282.8	1103.0	138.8	8083.1	315.0
1995	8269.4	287.5	1052.2	130.6	9321.6	304.5
1996	7941.3	262.9	945.7	81.0	8887.0	275.1
1997	9939.7	308.5	1026.1	91.2	10965.8	321.7
1998	9640.4	301.6	979.6	88.4	10620.0	314.3
1999	10805.7	344.5	957.5	100.6	11763.1	358.9
2000	9470.2	290.2	1031.1	85.3	10501.3	302.5
2001	7904.0	226.9	779.7	59.0	8683.7	234.5

[a] In thousands.

The optimization of hunting regulations for midcontinent mallards accounts for two other sources of uncertainty. Uncertainty about future environmental conditions is characterized by random variation in annual precipitation, which affects the number of ponds available during May in Canada. There also is an accounting for partial controllability, in which the link between regulations and harvest rates is imperfect due to uncontrollable factors (e.g., weather, timing of migration) that affect mallard harvest. A detailed description of the population dynamics of midcontinent mallards and associated sources of uncertainty are provided by Johnson et al. (1997) and in Appendix B.

A key component of the AHM process for midcontinent mallards is the annual updating of model weights via Bayes Theorem (Appendix C). These weights describe the relative ability of the alternative models to predict changes in population size, and they ultimately influence the nature of the optimal regulatory strategy. Model weights are based on a comparison of predicted and observed population sizes, with the updating leading to higher weights for models that prove to be good predictors (i.e., models with relatively small differences between predicted and observed population sizes) (Fig. 2). These comparisons account for sampling error (i.e., partial observability) in population size and pond counts, as well as for partial observability and controllability of harvest rates.

The AHM learning process based on Bayes Theorem is a logical, unbiased approach for discriminating among alternative models. It does, however, have its limitations. We must assume that the most appropriate model remains so over time, or that changes will be gradual enough that they can be recognized by shifts in model weights. Also, the rate at which model weights can change over time is dependent on the components of variation (or uncertainty) that are accounted for in the updating process. Not all sources of uncertainty are easily quantified, and their omission can lead to changes in model weights that are unrealistically rapid. Finally, and most importantly, the updating process determines only the relative ability of the alternative models to predict changes in population size. Any conclusions about the validity of the ecological mechanisms represented in the models (e.g., additive hunting mortality) are necessarily limited.

When the AHM process was initiated in 1995, the four alternative models of population dynamics were considered equally likely, reflecting a high degree of uncertainty (or disagreement) about harvest and environmental impacts on mallard abundance. Considering all years since 1995, the two models incorporating compensatory hunting mortality have been poor predictors of changes in population size (Table 2). Of the two remaining models, the model with strongly density-dependent reproduction has been strongly favored since last year.

7

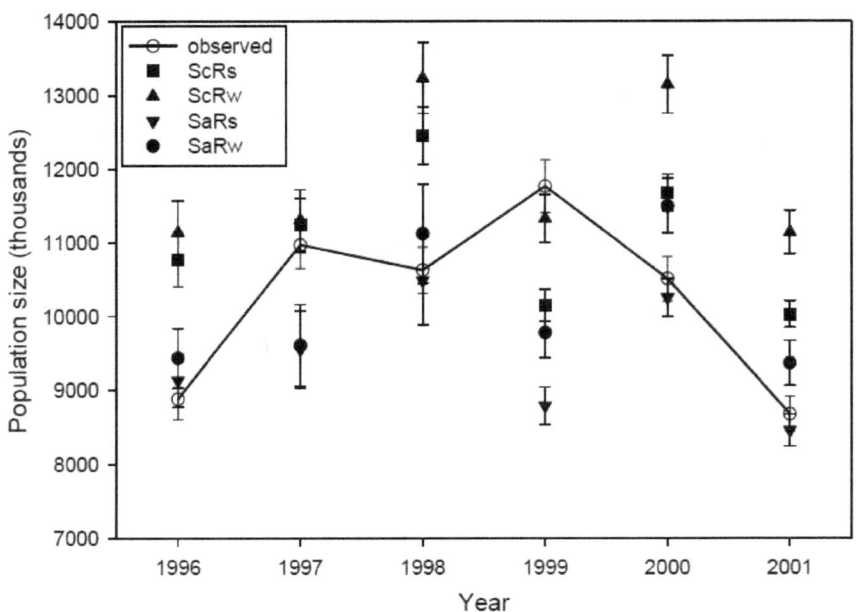

Fig. 2. Estimates of observed mallard population size (line with open circles) compared with predictions from four alternative models of population dynamics (ScRs = compensatory mortality and strongly density-dependent reproduction; ScRw = compensatory mortality and weakly density-dependent reproduction; SaRs = additive mortality and strongly density-dependent reproduction; SaRw = additive mortality and weakly density-dependent reproduction). Vertical bars represent one standard deviation on either side of the expected population size.

Table 2. Temporal changes in probabilities ("weights") for alternative hypotheses of midcontinent mallard population dynamics. Weights = 0.00001 represent minimum values imposed to prevent models from being eliminated from the model set.

Mortality hypothesis	Reproductive hypothesis	Model weights						
		1995	1996	1997	1998	1999	2000	2001
Additive	Strong density dependence	0.25000	0.65479	0.53015	0.61311	0.60883	0.91205	0.97466
Additive	Weak density dependence	0.25000	0.34514	0.46872	0.38687	0.38416	0.08793	0.02532
Compensatory	Strong density dependence	0.25000	0.00006	0.00112	0.00001	0.00001	0.00001	0.00001
Compensatory	Weak density dependence	0.25000	0.00001	0.00001	0.00001	0.00700	0.00001	0.00001

8

Eastern Mallards

For purposes of AHM, eastern mallards are defined as those breeding in southern Ontario and Quebec (federal survey strata 51-54 and 56) and in the northeastern U.S. (state plot surveys; Heusmann and Sauer 2000) (Fig. 1). Estimates of population size have varied from 856 thousand to 1.1 million during since 1990, with the majority of the population accounted for in the state surveys (Table 3).

Table 3. Estimates[a] of mallards breeding in the northeastern U.S. (state plot surveys) and eastern Canada (federal survey strata 51-54 and 56).

Year	State surveys		Federal surveys		Total	
	N	SE	N	SE	N	SE
1990	665.1	78.3	190.7	47.2	855.8	91.4
1991	779.2	88.3	152.8	33.7	932.0	94.5
1992	562.2	47.9	320.3	53.0	882.5	71.5
1993	683.1	49.7	292.1	48.2	975.2	69.3
1994	853.1	62.7	219.5	28.2	1072.5	68.7
1995	862.8	70.2	184.4	40.0	1047.2	80.9
1996	848.4	61.1	283.1	55.7	1131.5	82.6
1997	795.1	49.6	212.1	39.6	1007.2	63.4
1998	775.1	49.7	263.8	67.2	1038.9	83.6
1999	879.7	60.2	212.5	36.9	1092.2	70.6
2000	757.8	48.5	132.3	26.4	890.0	55.2
2001	807.5	51.4	200.2	35.6	1007.7	62.5

[a] In thousands.

The current model set for eastern mallards includes eight alternatives based on key uncertainties in reproductive and survival processes. This model set captures uncertainty about the relationship between fall age ratios (i.e., young/adult) and the Breeding Bird Survey (BBS) index, between the BBS index and actual population size as measured by federal and state surveys, and between the BBS index and natural-mortality rates of females (Table 10). All eight models are considered equally plausible given historic data. In constructing this model set we chose to focus on the nature of density-dependent population regulation because of its pivotal role in determining sustainable harvest strategies. However, there continues to be a need for a more comprehensive examination of environmental variables (e.g., precipitation) that might influence survival and reproductive rates irrespective of population size. Mathematical details of the alternative models for eastern mallards are provided in Appendix B and in *Adaptive Harvest Management for Eastern Mallards: Progress Report - January 13, 2000* (available online at http:\\www.migratorybirds.fws.gov/reports/reports.html).

Western Mallards

Western mallards have been defined as those breeding in the states of the Pacific Flyway (including Alaska), British Columbia, and the Yukon Territory. The distribution of these mallards during fall and winter is centered in the Pacific Flyway (Munro and Kimball 1982). Unfortunately, data-collection programs for understanding and monitoring the dynamics of this mallard stock are highly fragmented in both time and space. This fact is making it difficult to aggregate monitoring instruments in a way that can be used to reliably model this stock's dynamics and, thus, to establish criteria for regulatory decision-making under AHM. Another complicating factor is that federal survey strata 1-12 in Alaska and the Yukon are within the current geographic bounds of midcontinent mallards. Therefore, the AHM Working Group is continuing its investigations of western mallards, and hopes to recommend AHM protocols prior to the 2002 hunting season (see Current AHM Priorities later in this report).

HARVEST-MANAGEMENT OBJECTIVES

Midcontinent Mallards

The basic harvest-management objective for midcontinent mallards is to maximize cumulative harvest over the long term, which inherently requires perpetuation of the mallard population. Moreover, this objective is constrained to avoid regulations that could be expected to result in a subsequent population size below the goal of the North American Waterfowl Management Plan (NAWMP) (Fig. 3). According to this constraint, the value of harvest decreases proportionally as the difference between the goal and expected population size increases. This balance of harvest and population objectives results in a regulatory strategy that is more conservative than that for maximizing long-term harvest, but more liberal than a strategy to attain the NAWMP goal (regardless of effects on hunting opportunity). The current objective uses a population goal of 8.7 million mallards, which is based on the NAWMP goal of 8.1 million for the federal survey area and a goal 0.6 million for the combined states of Minnesota, Wisconsin, and Michigan.

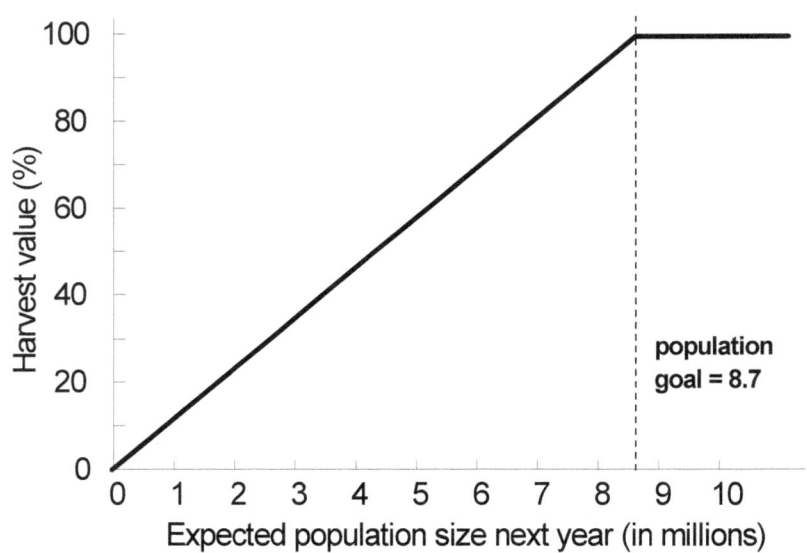

Fig. 3. The relative value of midcontinent mallard harvest, expressed as a function of breeding-population size expected in the subsequent year.

Eastern Mallards

The preliminary management objective for eastern mallards is to maximize long-term cumulative harvest. This objective is subject to change once the implications for average population size, variability in annual regulations, and other performance characteristics are better understood.

REGULATORY ALTERNATIVES

Evolution of Alternatives

When AHM was first implemented in 1995, three regulatory alternatives characterized as liberal, moderate, and restrictive were defined based on regulations used during 1979-84, 1985-87, and 1988-93, respectively (Appendix F, Table F-1). These regulatory alternatives also were considered for the 1996 hunting season. In 1997, the regulatory alternatives were modified to include: (1) the addition of a very restrictive alternative; (2) additional days and a higher duck bag-limit in the moderate and liberal alternatives; and (3) an increase in the bag limit of hen mallards in the moderate and liberal alternatives. The basic structure of the regulatory alternatives has remain unchanged since 1997, although in 1998 the U.S. Congress intervened to allow the option of extended framework dates and shorter seasons in some Mississippi Flyway States (Table 4).

Predictions of Mallard Harvest Rates

Since 1995, harvest rates of adult male mallards associated with the AHM regulatory alternatives have been predicted using harvest-rate estimates from 1979-84, which have been adjusted to reflect current specifications of season lengths and bag limits, and for contemporary numbers of hunters. These predictions are based only in part on band-recovery data, and rely heavily on models of hunting effort and success derived from hunter surveys (Appendix D). As such, these predictions have large sampling variances, and their accuracy is uncertain. Moreover, these predictions rely implicitly on an assumption that the historic relationship between hunting regulations (and harvest rates) in the U.S. and Canada will remain unchanged in the future. Currently, we have no way to judge whether this is a reasonable assumption. We also assumed that if hunting seasons were closed in the U.S., rates of harvest in Canada would be similar to those observed during 1988-93, which is the most recent period for which reliable estimates from Canada are available. This is a conservative approach given that we cannot be sure Canada would close its hunting season at the same time as the U.S. Fortunately, optimal regulatory strategies do not appear to be very sensitive to what we believe to be a realistic range of harvest-rate values associated with closed seasons in the U.S.

Predicted harvest rates of adult male mallards associated with each of the regulatory alternatives are provided in Tables 5 and 6 and Figs. 4 and 5. We made the simplifying assumption that the harvest rate of midcontinent mallards depends solely on the regulatory choice in the western three Flyways. This appears to be a reasonable assumption given the the small proportion of midcontinent mallards wintering in the Atlantic Flyway (Munro and Kimball 1982), and harvest-rate predictions that suggest a minimal effect of Atlantic Flyway regulations (U.S. Fish and Wildlife Service 2000). Under this assumption, the optimal regulatory strategy for the western three Flyways can be derived by ignoring the harvest regulations imposed in the Atlantic Flyway. However, the harvest rate of eastern mallards is affected significantly by regulatory choices beyond the Atlantic Flyway (U.S. Fish and Wildlife Service 2000). To avoid making the regulatory choice in the Atlantic Flyway conditional on regulations elsewhere, we estimated the expected harvest rates of eastern mallards when managers lack *a priori* knowledge of the regulation chosen in the western three Flyways. We did this by taking a weighted average of the estimated harvest rates associated with each of the possible regulatory alternatives in the western Flyways, for each possible regulatory alternative in the Atlantic Flyway. The weights were derived using simulations of the midcontinent-mallard harvest strategy to determine the expected frequency of regulatory choices in the western Flyways.

Adult female mallards tend to be less vulnerable to harvest than adult males, while young of both sexes are more vulnerable (Table 7). Estimates of the relative vulnerability of adult females and young in the eastern mallard population tend to be higher and more variable than in the midcontinent population.

Table 4. Regulatory alternatives for the 2001 duck-hunting season.

| Regulation | Flyway | | | |
	Atlantic[a]	Mississippi[b]	Central[c]	Pacific[d]
Shooting hours	one-half hour before sunrise to sunset for all Flyways			
Framework dates	Oct 1 - Jan 20	Saturday closest to October 1 - Sunday closest to January 20		
Season length (days)				
Very restrictive	20	20	25	38
Restrictive	30	30	39	60
Moderate	45	45	60	86
Liberal	60	60	74	107
Bag limit (total / mallard / female mallard)				
Very restrictive	3 / 3 / 1	3 / 2 / 1	3 / 3 / 1	4 / 3 / 1
Restrictive	3 / 3 / 1	3 / 2 / 1	3 / 3 / 1	4 / 3 / 1
Moderate	6 / 4 / 2	6 / 4 / 1	6 / 5 / 1	7 / 5 / 2
Liberal	6 / 4 / 2	6 / 4 / 2	6 / 5 / 2	7 / 7 / 2

[a] The states of Maine, Massachusetts, Connecticut, Pennsylvania, New Jersey, Maryland, Delaware, West Virginia, Virginia, and North Carolina are permitted to exclude Sundays, which are closed to hunting, from their total allotment of season days.
[b] In the states of Alabama, Mississippi, and Tennessee, in the moderate and liberal alternatives, the framework closing date is January 31 and season lengths are 38 days and 51 days, respectively.
[c] The High Plains Mallard Management Unit is allowed 8, 12, 23, and 23 extra days under the very restrictive, restrictive, moderate, and liberal alternatives, respectively.
[d] The Columbia Basin Mallard Management Unit is allowed seven extra days under the very restrictive, restrictive, and moderate alternatives.

Table 5. Predicted harvest rates of adult male midcontinent mallards under current regulatory alternatives for the three western Flyways (assuming a negligible effect of Atlantic Flyway regulations).

	Harvest rate	SE
Closed (U.S.)	0.0088	0.0030
Very restrictive	0.0526	0.0106
Restrictive	0.0665	0.0142
Moderate	0.1114	0.0266
Liberal	0.1305	0.0323

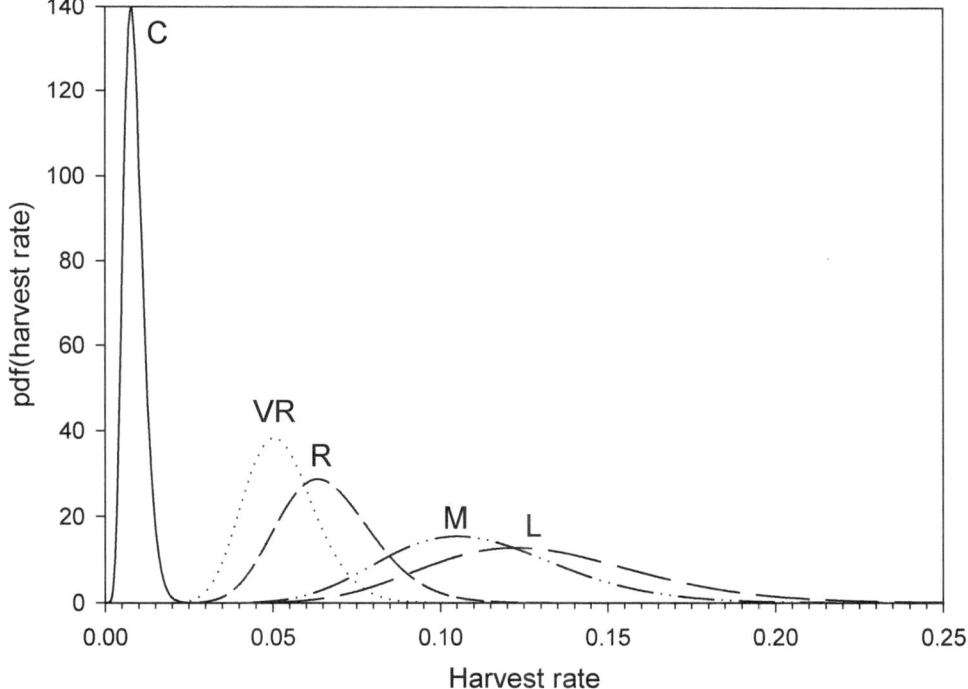

Fig. 4. Probability density functions (pdf) of harvest rates of adult male midcontinent mallards under current regulatory alternatives in the three western Flyways. (C = closed in U.S., VR = very restrictive, R = restrictive, M = moderate, L = liberal)

Table 6. Predicted harvest rates of adult male eastern mallards under current regulatory alternatives for the Atlantic Flyway, based on expected frequencies of regulatory choices in the three western Flyways.

	Harvest rate	SE
Closed (U.S.)	0.1100	0.0135
Very restrictive	0.1382	0.0205
Restrictive	0.1488	0.0223
Moderate	0.1661	0.0258
Liberal	0.1756	0.0278

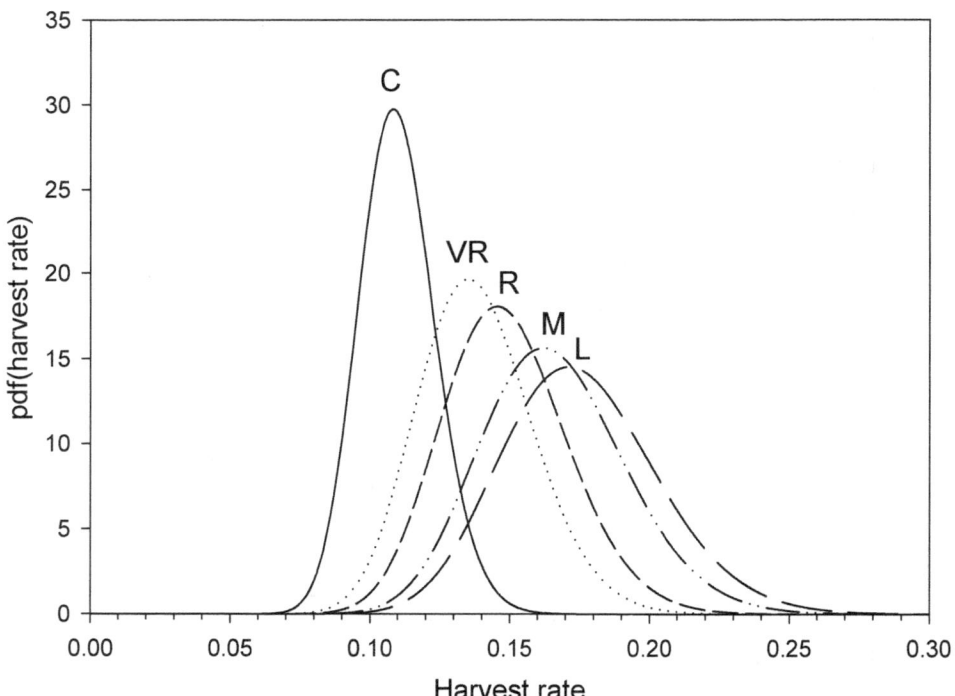

Fig. 5. Probability density functions (pdf) of harvest rates of adult male eastern mallards, under current regulatory alternatives in the Atlantic Flyway. (C = closed in U.S., VR = very restrictive, R = restrictive, M = moderate, L = liberal)

Table 7. Mean harvest vulnerability (SE) of adult female and young mallards, relative to adult males, based on band-recovery data, 1979-95.

Mallard population	Age and sex		
	Adult females	Young females	Young males
Midcontinent	0.748 (0.108)	1.188 (0.138)	1.361 (0.144)
Eastern	0.985 (0.145)	1.320 (0.264)	1.449 (0.211)

OPTIMAL REGULATORY STRATEGIES

We continue to use a constrained approach to the optimization of midcontinent and eastern mallard harvests. Rather than a joint-optimization approach, we based the Atlantic Flyway regulatory strategy exclusively on the status of eastern mallards, and the regulatory strategy for the remaining Flyways exclusively on the status of midcontinent mallards. This approach was first used last year, and continues to be considered provisional until its implications for the harvests of multiple mallard stocks and other species are better understood.

The optimal regulatory strategy for the three western Flyways was derived using: (1) current regulatory alternatives; (2) the four alternative models and associated weights for midcontinent mallards; and (3) the dual objectives to maximize long-term cumulative harvest and achieve a population goal of 8.7 million midcontinent mallards. The resulting regulatory strategy (Table 8) is slightly more liberal than that in 2000, due to the increase in probability associated with the hypothesis of strongly density-dependent reproduction. The optimal regulatory strategies based on midcontinent mallards for the 1995-00 seasons are provided in Appendix F (Tables F-2 to F-7) so that the reader can assess how the regulatory strategy has "evolved" over time. Blank cells in Table 8 (and in other strategies in this report) represent resource conditions that are insufficient to support an open season in the U.S., given current regulatory alternatives and harvest-management objectives.

We simulated the use of the regulatory strategy in Table 8 with the four population models and current weights to determine expected performance characteristics. Assuming that regulatory choices adhered to this strategy, the harvest value and breeding-population size would be expected to average 1.3 (SD = 0.4) million and 8.0 (SD = 1.0) million, respectively.

Based on a midcontinent population size of 8.7 million mallards (federal surveys plus state surveys in MN, MI, and WI) and 2.7 million ponds in Prairie Canada, the optimal regulatory choice for the Pacific, Central, and Mississippi Flyways in 2001 is the liberal alternative.

As last year, we optimized the regulatory choice for the Atlantic Flyway based on: (1) current regulatory alternatives; (2) the eight alternative models of eastern-mallard population dynamics; and (3) an objective to maximize long-term cumulative harvest. We were unable to update the weights for the eastern-mallard models due to uncertainty about recent changes in band-reporting rate, and because of a suspected bias in the BBS index (see Current AHM Priorities later in this report). Therefore, the optimal regulatory strategy for the Atlantic Flyway continues to be based on equal weights for the eight eastern-mallard models.

The resulting regulatory strategy suggests liberal regulations for all population sizes of record, and is characterized by a lack of intermediate regulations (Table 9). The strategy exhibits this behavior largely because of the small differences in harvest rate among regulatory alternatives (Table 6, Fig. 5).

We simulated the use of the regulatory strategy in Table 9 to determine expected performance characteristics. Assuming that harvest management adhered to this strategy, the annual harvest and breeding population size would be expected to average 387 (SD = 99) thousand and 1.06 (SD = 0.2) million, respectively.

Based on a breeding population size of 1.0 million mallards, the optimal regulatory choice for the Atlantic Flyway in 2001 is the liberal alternative.

Table 8. Optimal regulatory choices[a] in the three western Flyways for the 2001 hunting season. This strategy is based on current regulatory alternatives, on current midcontinent-mallard models and weights, and on the dual objectives of maximizing long-term cumulative harvest and achieving a population goal of 8.7 million mallards.

	Ponds[b]									
Mallards[c]	1.5	2.0	2.5	3.0	3.5	4.0	4.5	5.0	5.5	6.0
<4.5										
4.5										VR
5.0					VR	VR	VR	VR	R	R
5.5	VR	VR	VR	VR	R	R	R	M	M	M
6.0	R	R	R	R	M	M	M	M	L	L
6.5	R	R	M	M	M	L	L	L	L	L
7.0	M	M	M	L	L	L	L	L	L	L
7.5	M	L	L	L	L	L	L	L	L	L
8.0	L	L	L	L	L	L	L	L	L	L
>8.0	L	L	L	L	L	L	L	L	L	L

[a] VR = very restrictive, R = restrictive, M = moderate, and L = liberal.
[b] Estimated number of ponds in Prairie Canada in May, in millions.
[c] Estimated number of midcontinent mallards during May, in millions.

Table 9. Optimal regulatory choices[a] in the Atlantic Flyway for the 2001 hunting season. This strategy is based on current regulatory alternatives, on eight alternative models of eastern mallards (equally weighted), and on an objective to maximize long-term cumulative harvest.

Mallards[b]	Regulation
<500	
500	R
550	L
>550	L

[a] VR = very restrictive, R = restrictive, M = moderate, and L = liberal.
[b] Estimated number of eastern mallards in the combined federal and state surveys, in thousands.

CURRENT AHM PRIORITIES
Strategic Considerations in AHM

The AHM Working Group has begun a strategic discussion about future development of AHM. This discussion was motivated in part by the special session on AHM that was held at the 2000 North American Wildlife and Natural Resources Conference (Humburg et al. 2000, Johnson and Case 2000, Nichols 2000). That session offered a retrospective on the development of AHM, and described both technical and institutional issues affecting future progress. Discussions are focused on the following questions:

(1)   Is harvest an appropriate performance metric (i.e., basis of a management objective)? If so, should we also set explicit goals for harvest allocation? If not harvest, then what is the appropriate metric, how is it related to regulations and population dynamics, and how would it be monitored?

(2)   Under what conditions do we need to establish goals for population size? How should these goals be traded off against hunting opportunity?

(3)   Should learning be pursued more aggressively (i.e., should we move from passive to active adaptive management)?

(4)   What are appropriate criteria (e.g., number, range, empirical basis) for establishing or revising the set of regulatory alternatives?

(5)   How should we apply the principles of AHM to species/populations for which there is little basis for constructing predictive models?

(6)   What are appropriate criteria for establishing a set of alternative models (i.e., how do we determine "key uncertainties")?

(7)   What are the appropriate temporal, spatial, and organizational scales of harvest management (i.e., to what degree do we account for these sources of variation in population dynamics)? How do we distinguish what is desirable from what is practical?

A white paper describing these strategic issues and possible future directions will be prepared for review by the AHM Working Group.

Midcontinent Mallards

The models used to set hunting regulations for midcontinent mallards have been in place since 1995. Over the last six years, the model structure, model set, and model weights have been under constant scrutiny and review by parties internal and external to the AHM process. As various concerns have emerged, the AHM Working Group has recommended against making piecemeal changes, instead preferring to make a number of changes at once. Enough insight has now amassed to allow a comprehensive revision of the model set and weights.

There are three primary concerns about the current AHM models for midcontinent mallards: (1) the overall model structure; (2) the set of reproductive and survival sub-models; and (3) the methods used to update model weights.

Model structure.–The four alternative models share a common structure that relates changes in population size (N) to recruitment (R) and age- and sex-specific survival (S). The four alternative models differ at the sub-model level, in the way that R and S depend on the state and decision variables. Currently, the models all assume that the general structure (i.e., the "balance equation") is unbiased and perfectly precise. However, there is strong evidence to the contrary. We have yearly estimates of all three components of the balance equation: each year (t), N is estimated from the May breeding-population survey, R is estimated from the harvest age ratios and band-recovery data, and S is estimated for each age (a) and sex (s) class using banding data. In theory, then, N_t, R_t, and $S_{a, s, t}$ should perfectly predict N_{t+1}. In fact, they do not. Martin et al. (1979) found that the balance equation over-predicted N_{t+1} by about 25%, and the bias appears to be of about the same magnitude in more recent years. These results are consistent with the hypothesis that estimated survival rates, recruitment rates, or both are positively biased. The source and cause of the bias is not known. It is worth noting, however, that this bias in the balance equation is seen in other stocks as well (e.g., eastern mallards, northern pintails).

Reproductive and survival sub-models.--There has been considerable discussion about whether the current model set appropriately captures uncertainty about population dynamics and the effects of harvest. This has lead to consideration of substitutions and additions to the model set.

In both current models of reproduction (weakly and strongly density-dependent), reproductive rate (fall age ratio) is a linear function of breeding-population size and May ponds. The two alternatives differ in the parameter values of the linear model, having been chosen on theoretical grounds from the likelihood profile. Two concerns have been raised about these models. First, large-scale landscape changes, like agriculture and the Conservation Reserve Program, could be affecting recruitment (Miller 2000). If so, a temporal component should be added to the reproductive sub-model, or these landscape effects should be included explicitly. Second, recent theoretical work (Runge and Johnson 2001) has emphasized the importance of functional form on solutions of optimal control problems, suggesting alternatives to a linear model should be considered.

The survival sub-models express two alternatives about the effects of harvest. The sub-model expressing additive hunting mortality is viewed as a natural and reasonable hypothesis. The primary concern has been with the phenomenological compensatory sub-model (Johnson et al. 1993). This sub-model treats annual survival as a function of harvest rate, with increases in harvest rate to a threshold being compensated by decreases in non-harvest mortality, so that for low harvest rates annual survival is constant. The problem is that this sub-model does not incorporate any biological mechanism for compensation. The mechanism suspected for compensation is density-dependent mortality, suggesting that post-harvest survival should be a negative function of post-harvest population density. In this case, harvest mortality would be expected to be largely additive at low population densities and at least partially compensatory at high densities. Thus, the current sub-model identified as the best predictor of annual survival is likely to change with population density. Because of concerns about the ability of model weights to track these changes over time, a more mechanistic "compensatory" model probably should be developed.

Updating model weights.--The purpose of updating model weights in the adaptive setting is to identify the model providing the most accurate predictions over time, based on a comparison of the observed breeding-population size with the those predicted under each alternative model. Two results of the model-weight updating over the past six years have been surprising: (1) model weights have shifted relatively quickly to a single model (97% of the weight on the SaRs model in 2001); and (2) the model weights have changed dramatically in some years. There is growing suspicion that the first result is due to the bias in the balance equation discussed above. The second result is likely due to variances in model predictions that are under-estimated. These two problems need to be addressed to ensure that the updating procedure provides stronger inferences about appropriate models and is more reflective of actual rates of learning.

The AHM Working Group has assigned a small committee of state and federal technicians to work on revisions to the model set and updating procedures for midcontinent mallards. The committee plans to have its analyses and recommendations available to interested parties by January 2002.

Eastern Mallards

The AHM Working Group also is exploring whether major revisions to the model set for eastern mallards (Table 10) may be warranted prior to the next regulatory cycle. There are several reasons why revisions may be appropriate. First, a reduction in the number of models may be possible because differences in model-specific regulatory strategies are minor (Table 11). This result is due in part to the large variances associated with regulation-specific harvest rates (Table 6, Fig. 5).

Table 10. The model set for eastern mallards, in which sub-models are permitted to assume alternative functional forms.[a]

| | Submodel | | |
Model designation	R = f(BBS)	BBS = f(N)	••
r1b1s1	negative exponential	logarithmic	normal random variable
r1b1s2	negative exponential	logarithmic	• •= f(BBS)
r1b2s1	negative exponential	exponential rise to maximum	normal random variable
r1b2s2	negative exponential	exponential rise to maximum	• •= f(BBS)
r2b1s1	logistic	logarithmic	normal random variable
r2b1s2	logistic	logarithmic	• •= f(BBS)
r2b2s1	logistic	exponential rise to maximum	normal random variable
r2b2s2	logistic	exponential rise to maximum	• •= f(BBS)

[a] R = fall age ratio, BBS = Breeding Bird Survey index, and • •= summer survival of adult females.

Another motivation for revising the model set concerns the tendency for empirical estimates of survival and reproductive rates to imply annual population growth rates that are higher than those observed in the BBS index (Fig. 6). The amount of over-prediction in population size (as based on the BBS index) averages about 30%, suggesting a positive bias in estimated survival rates, reproductive rates, or both. Correcting for this bias makes regulatory strategies more conservative, but the degree of conservatism depends on the specific population model, and whether the bias is assumed to reside in the survival rates or in the reproductive rates. Fortunately, the optimal regulatory decision in the Atlantic Flyway would have not been any different last year had we been aware of the apparent bias in predicted growth rate. With respect to future regulatory decisions, however, we believe it will be important to admit the possibility of a significant positive bias in predicted growth rates.

Yet another issue involves the possibility of a systematic error in the BBS. We have discovered that the rate at which eastern-mallard population growth is over-predicted is positively related to spring precipitation in the northeastern U.S. (Fig. 7). This finding is consistent with the hypothesis that the BBS index is biased low in years of high precipitation, perhaps because of an unrecognized decline in observers' ability to detect birds. The regulatory implications of such a bias are not yet clear, but the problem might be avoided by relying on estimates of population size derived from the state and federal waterfowl surveys for all aspects of eastern-mallard modeling. New problems arise in this approach, however, as there are far fewer years in which these surveys have been conducted when compared to the BBS. Nonetheless, rejection of the BBS in favor of the statistically designed federal and state surveys is almost certainly the best long-term solution.

Table 11. Optimal regulatory choices in the Atlantic Flyway for each alternative model of eastern mallards, conditioned on current regulatory alternatives and an objective to maximize long-term cumulative harvest.[a] Model descriptions are provided in Table 10.

N	Model designation							
	r1b2s1	r1b2s2	r1b1s1	r2b2s1	r1b1s2	r2b2s2	r2b1s1	r2b1s2
50	C	C	C	C	C	C	C	C
100	C	C	C	C	C	C	C	C
150	C	C	C	C	C	C	C	C
200	C	C	C	C	C	C	C	C
250	C	C	C	C	C	C	C	C
300	C	C	C	C	C	C	C	C
350	C	C	C	C	C	C	C	C
400	C	C	C	C	C	C	C	R
450	C	C	C	C	C	R	R	L
500	C	C	C	R	M	L	L	L
550	C	C	VR	L	L	L	L	L
600	C	VR	R	L	L	L	L	L
650	C	M	L	L	L	L	L	L
700	C	L	L	L	L	L	L	L
750	C	L	L	L	L	L	L	L
800	C	L	L	L	L	L	L	L
850	VR	L	L	L	L	L	L	L
900	R	L	L	L	L	L	L	L
950	M	L	L	L	L	L	L	L
1000	L	L	L	L	L	L	L	L
1050	L	L	L	L	L	L	L	L
1100	L	L	L	L	L	L	L	L

[a] N = breeding population size (in thousands) as measured by state and federal surveys. C = closed in the U.S., VR = very restrictive, R = restrictive, M = moderate, L = liberal.

Finally, any revision of the model set for eastern mallards is inevitably linked to the development of an AHM process for American black ducks (*Anas rubripes*). Hunting regulations for eastern mallards and black ducks cannot be considered independently because there is evidence that black duck productivity is reduced in the presence of mallards. Thus, regulatory decisions for mallards can affect the status, and therefore the harvest, of black ducks. There also is an inherent regulatory dependency because both black ducks and mallards are exposed to a common harvest through hunting seasons established for all duck species. The relationship between black duck and mallard harvest management is being considered by the Black Duck AHM Working Group. Information about the activities of this group is available online at http://fisher.forestry.uga.edu/blackduck.

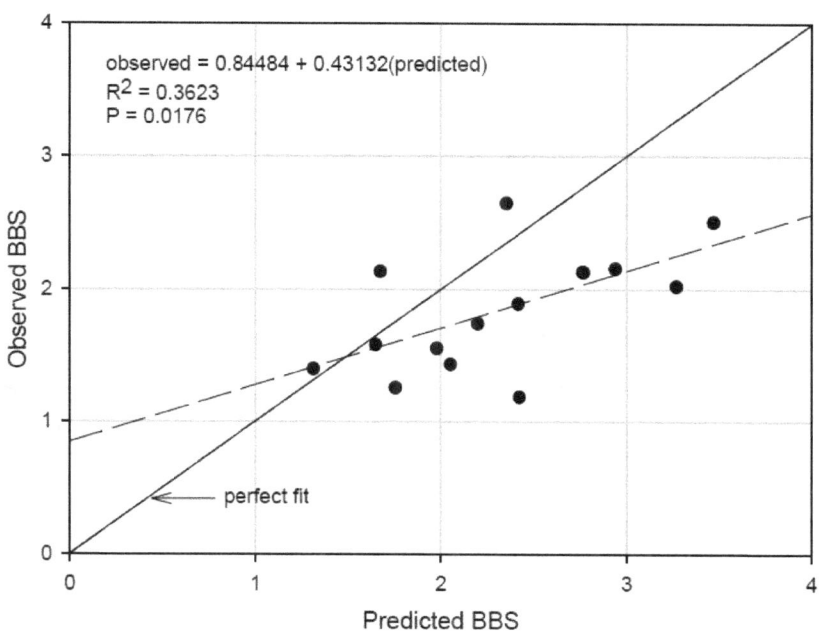

Fig. 6. The relationship between the observed and predicted BBS index for eastern mallards based on empirical estimates of survival and reproductive rates.

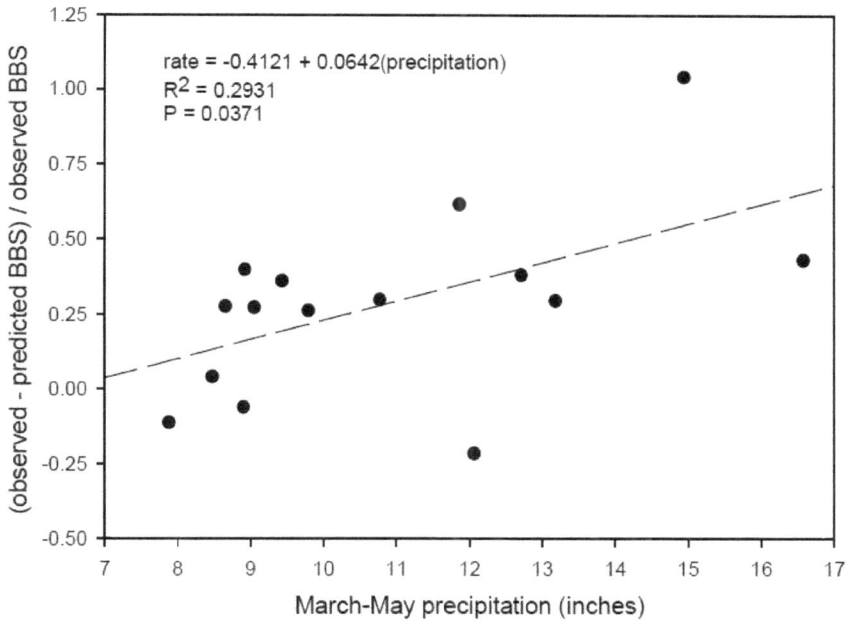

Fig. 7. The rate of over-prediction in eastern mallard growth rates as a function of spring precipitation in the northeastern U.S.

Western Mallards

The AHM Working Group, in cooperation with the Study Committee of Pacific Flyway Council, is continuing its efforts to incorporate western mallards in the AHM framework. Recent investigations have focused on: (1) management implications of a western-mallard models developed by the New York Cooperative Fish and Wildlife Research Unit; and (2) deriving joint harvest strategies for western and midcontinent mallards (i.e., those that allow Flyway-specific regulatory choices depending on mallard derivations). Based on currently available stock-specific models, the optimal harvest rates (on adult males) for maximizing harvest under average environmental conditions are 0.19 and 0.45 for midcontinent and western mallards, respectively. Despite this difference in optimal harvest rates, there appears to be only a 1% gain in expected harvest from a joint strategy for midcontinent and western mallards compared to a harvest strategy based on midcontinent mallards alone.

A number of concerns about the models for western mallards have surfaced in the course of this investigation, however. Most importantly, the models predict changes in population size that are biased high and are uncorrelated with observed population changes based on the BBS. The bias in predicted population size may be the result of a positive bias in estimated survival or reproductive rates, as is suspected in other duck stocks. However, the fact that predicted changes in western-mallard population size were uncorrelated with observed changes is also worrisome. The reason for a lack of correlation may involve the mix of spatial and temporal domains of scale that were used to generate estimates of reproductive and survival rates of western mallards. Another possibility involves the reliability of the BBS index, which is only weakly related to aerial surveys of mallards in most Pacific Flyway States.

In conclusion, the currently available models of western mallards do not appear to provide an acceptable basis for implementing a joint harvest strategy with midcontinent mallards. The AHM Working Group currently is re-examining all available data on population sizes, and re-estimating vital rates that are more coincident in time and space. It should be recognized, however, that available data on population size and vital rates are sparse, and this may prevent (at least initially) the inclusion of some breeding areas currently considered part of the western-mallard breeding range.

Northern Pintails

An adaptive harvest management program for pintails has been evolving over the past three years, and it is possible that the details of implementing such a program may be worked out by next year. In order for an AHM program to be implemented for pintails, however, several issues need to be resolved.

Two of the most important issues are value-based, are not unique to pintails, and may have a bearing on how other stocks are included in AHM. First, *how will decisions about pintail harvest interact with decisions about mallard harvest?* Alternatives include: (1) pintail and mallard harvest regulations are set independently (i.e., species-specific season lengths and bag limits); (2) bag limits are allowed to vary between pintails and mallards, but the species share a season length determined by their joint population status; and (3) pintail bag limits are set conditionally upon a season length determined solely by mallard status. The second question involves the relationship between pintail harvest management and the population goal of the North American Waterfowl Management Plan. Specifically, *how much should we forego harvest opportunity to allow population recovery?* At the heart of this question is the concern that the pintail population has been in decline for the past 30 years. The recent Northern Pintail Workshop (Sacramento, CA, March 23-25, 2001) focused on articulating the hypotheses and evaluating the evidence for the decline. While there seems to be little concern that harvest is the primary cause of the decline, it is possible that harvest is hindering recovery.

There also are two key technical challenges to the implementation of AHM for pintails. First, there is an apparent negative bias in the estimate of breeding-population size in years when pintails settle in more northerly areas (due to dry conditions in the prairies). Second, empirical estimates of reproductive and survival rates imply rates of annual population growth that are about 30% higher on average than those derived from the breeding-population survey. Both of these problems arise from biases in pintail monitoring programs, but the exact nature and cause of the biases are unknown. Efforts are underway to identify possible causal explanations, and it may be possible to implement an empirical correction for these biases.

AHM and Considerations of Hunter Preferences

In spite of significant progress in defining harvest-management objectives, there continue to be unresolved disagreements among stakeholders about how to value harvest benefits and how those benefits should be shared. Resolution of these disagreements might be facilitated by a better understanding of how regulations affect hunter satisfaction. Most Flyway Council members have expressed an interest in coordinated, nationwide hunter surveys to monitor the opinions of waterfowl hunters. Despite agreement on the need for better data, however, the specific use and application of these data in the AHM process remain unclear. Therefore, a subcommittee of the AHM working group was appointed to discuss how to proceed on this issue. The subcommittee is attempting to assemble experts in both harvest management and human dimensions to frame the issue and suggest options for proceeding. The recommendations of this group will be compiled for distribution and review among various interests.

Information and Education Needs

Information and education efforts are critical to the continued success of AHM. Recently, however, the AHM Working Group has become concerned that the technical complexity of AHM may be preventing some waterfowl managers from fully participating in the review and development of AHM procedures. The AHM Working Group is taking a number of actions to address this concern. First, an AHM training workshop was held December 5-6, 2000 at the National Wetlands Research Center in Lafayette, Louisiana. The purpose of the workshop was to enhance the understanding of AHM by biologists directly involved in the regulatory process, and to help those biologists communicate AHM concepts and practices to their peers and constituents. The training workshop was attended by 25 federal and state biologists, and consisted of lectures and exercises covering harvest theory, population modeling, decision theory, and Bayesian learning. Additionally, the AHM Working Group is preparing a short presentation that can be used to educate administrators about the basic concepts of AHM.

The Need for a Reward-Band Study

The AHM Working Group is increasingly concerned about the ability of AHM to function as intended without updated estimates of band-reporting rates (i.e., the rate at which hunters report band recoveries of their own volition). Therefore, the AHM Working Group recently issued the following position statement to help strengthen the justification for the conduct of a reward-band study:

"Adaptive Harvest Management (AHM) was implemented by the U.S. Fish and Wildlife Service (FWS) in 1995 in an effort to better link data from monitoring programs to harvest-regulations decisions for ducks. Over the past decade, Federal and State biologists have made extensive use of the information from operational surveys designed to assess duck abundance, production and harvest. As a result, several models of population dynamics for various stocks of ducks (e.g., mid-continent mallards, eastern mallards, northern pintails) have been developed to better manage harvests of these birds.

The North American Waterfowl Banding Program is an essential component of these efforts. Waterfowl are live-trapped, banded, and released annually, and a proportion of these banded birds are subsequently harvested by hunters. The band-reporting rate (i.e., the proportion of bands from hunter-shot birds that are reported to the Bird Banding Laboratory [BBL]) is required to estimate several parameters essential to model population dynamics. For example, the reporting rate is used in conjunction with recovery rates (i.e., the proportion of the banded birds that is shot and retrieved by hunters each year) to yield information about the harvest rate on populations. Additionally, the harvest rate of immature birds relative to that of adult birds is used in conjunction with harvest age-ratio data (derived from harvest surveys) to estimate the annual recruitment rate of waterfowl. Precise estimates for these two parameters (i.e., harvest rate and production) are critical to the AHM Working Group's efforts to develop useful population models. The AHM process is compromised when these parameters cannot be estimated accurately and precisely.

Historically, estimates of the band-reporting rates for mallards suggested that only about one-third of banded mallards shot and retrieved by hunters were reported to the BBL; rates for other species are unknown. In an effort to improve the cost-effectiveness of the banding program and to provide more precise information to help refine waterfowl management, managers in the FWS, the Canadian Wildlife Service, and the Flyways devised a strategic plan to increase reporting rates. The plan included changing inscriptions on the bands to include a toll-free telephone number by which hunters could report the bands. Unfortunately, a necessary drawback to changing band inscriptions entails enduring a period of time during which reporting rates would be changing and uncertain, thus precluding direct estimation of harvest and recruitment rates.

Beginning in 1995, bands with the toll-free number were placed on mallards. Since that time, reports of bands to the BBL via the toll-free number have increased from about 14% to 92% of all reports. Results of a small-scale pilot study (using only adult male mallards in a restricted geographic area) conducted during 1998-2000 suggest that reporting rates of toll-free bands for that cohort have stabilized over the last 3 years at about 80%. Although these results suggest that changing to toll-free bands may have doubled reporting rates, earlier studies indicate that band-reporting rates for mallards vary geographically and perhaps by gender of birds. Thus, using reporting rates from this small-scale study to estimate harvest and recruitment rates of mallards would be imprudent.

In addition to its efforts to refine the AHM process for mallards, the Working Group has been asked to assess other issues related to harvest management as AHM has evolved. For example, the Working Group has been asked to assess the potential effects of framework-date extensions on optimal harvest strategies. In those assessments, we stated that we are unsure how the extensions would affect harvest rates, due to extremely limited and dated experience with such extensions. The assessments are based on information that is at least a decade old, before changes in reporting rates due to altering band inscriptions occurred. An adequate assessment of the effects of framework-date extensions on optimal harvest strategies would require contemporary estimates of harvest rates, which in turn require contemporary estimates of reporting rates.

Also, there is a strong desire by stakeholders to include other species (e.g., wood ducks, black ducks, geese) into the AHM process. For some species, band-recovery data are the primary source of information for developing appropriate management recommendations. Managers believe that demographics of hunters harvesting these various stocks are sufficiently different to cause reporting rates to differ from those estimated for mallards. Thus, using reporting rates specific to mallards would not adequately address needs related to modeling and monitoring efforts for these other stocks of birds.

Given these arguments, it is the position of the AHM Working Group that a large-scale reward-band study is absolutely critical to assess the ramifications of changing regulatory alternatives (e.g., altering framework dates, season lengths, bag limits). Further, such a study would provide us with contemporary information necessary to refine the AHM process for mallards, and would enhance the possibility of using the AHM process for managing other stocks of waterfowl. Results from the pilot study suggest that reporting rates likely have stabilized at a new, higher rate. Thus, we believe it is time to move forward with a full-scale reward-band study that (1) encompasses a greater geographic area for mallards, (2) can detect whether reporting rates differ between males and female mallards, and (3) can assess whether reporting rates differ among stocks of waterfowl. Without contemporary estimates of reporting rates for the new toll-free bands, we cannot conduct adequate assessments for the issues with which we have been tasked."

LITERATURE CITED

Anderson, , D. R., and C. J. Henny. 1972. Population ecology of the mallard. I. A review of previous studies and the   distribut

Blohm, R. J. 1989. Introduction to harvest - understanding surveys and season setting. Proc. Inter. Waterfowl Symp. 6:118- 133.

Burnham, K. P., G. C. White, and D. R. Anderson. 1984. Estimating the effect of hunting on annual survival rates of adult   mallards. J. Wildl. Manage. 48:350-361.

Heusman, H W, and J. R. Sauer. 2000. The northeastern state's waterfowl breeding population survey. The Wildl. Soc. Bull. 28:355-364.

Humburg, D. D., T. W. Aldrich, S. Baker, G. Costanzo, J. H. Gammonley, M. A. Johnson, B. Swift, and D. Yparraguirre.. 2000. Adaptive harvest management: has anything really changed? Trans. North Am. Wildl. Nat. Resour. Conf. 65:78-93.

Johnson, F. A., and D. J. Case. 2000. Adaptive regulation of waterfowl harvests: lessons learned and prospects for the future. Trans. North Am. Wildl. Nat. Resour. Conf. 65:94-108.

_____, C. T. Moore, W. L. Kendall, J. A. Dubovsky, D. F. Caithamer, J. R. Kelley, Jr., and B. K. Williams. 1997. Uncertainty and the management of mallard harvests. J. Wildl. Manage. 61:202-216.

_____, B. K. Williams, J. D. Nichols, J. E. Hines, W. L. Kendall, G. W. Smith, and D. F. Caithamer. 1993. Developing an adaptive management strategy for harvesting waterfowl in North America. Trans. North Am. Wildl. Nat. Resour. Conf. 58:565-583.

_____, _____, and P. R. Schmidt. 1996. Adaptive decision-making in waterfowl harvest and habitat management. Proc. Inter. Waterfowl Symp. 7:26-33.

Martin, F. W., R. S. Pospahala, and J. D. Nichols. 1979. Assessment and population management of North American migratory birds. Pages 187-239 *in* J. Cairns, Jr., G. P. Patil, and W. E. Waters, eds. Environmental biomonitoring, assessment, prediction, and management - certain case studies and related quantitative issues. Inter. Coop. Publ. House, Fairland, MD.

Miller, M. W. 2000. Modeling annual mallard production in the prairie-parkland region. J. Wildl. Manage. 64:561-575.

Munro, R. E., and C. F. Kimball. 1982. Population ecology of the mallard. VII. Distribution and derivation of the harvest. U.S. Fish and Wildl. Serv. Resour. Pub. 147. 127pp.

Nichols, J. D. 2000. Evolution of harvest management for North American waterfowl: selective pressures and preadaptations for adaptive harvest management. Trans. North Am. Wildl. Nat. Resour. Conf. 65:65-77.

Nichols, J. D., F. A. Johnson, and B. K. Williams. 1995. Managing North American waterfowl in the face of uncertainty. Ann. Rev. Ecol. Syst. 26:177-199.

Runge, M. C. and F. A. Johnson. 2001. The importance of functional form in optimal control solutions of problems in population dynamics. Ecol. *In press.*

Schafer, J. L. 1997. Analysis of incomplete multivariate data. Chapman and Hall, London. 430pp.

U.S. Fish and Wildlife Service. 2000. Adaptive harvest management: 2000 Hunting season. U.S. Dept. Interior, Washington. D.C. 43pp.

Walters, C. J. 1986. Adaptive management of renewable resources. MacMillan Publ. Co., New York, N.Y. 374pp.

Williams, B. K., and F. A. Johnson. 1995. Adaptive management and the regulation of waterfowl harvests. Wildl. Soc. Bull. 23:430-436.

_____, _____, and K. Wilkins. 1996. Uncertainty and the adaptive management of waterfowl harvests. J. Wildl. Manage. 60:223-232.

APPENDIX A: AHM Working Group

Bob Blohm
U.S. Fish and Wildlife Service
Arlington Square, Room 634
4401 North Fairfax Drive,
Arlington, VA 22203
phone: 703-358-1966
fax: 703-358-2272
e-mail: robert_blohm@fws.gov

Scott Baker
Dept. of Wildlife, Fisheries, & Parks
P.O. Box 378
Redwood, MS 39156
 phone: 601-661-0294
fax: 601-364-2209
e-mail: mahannah1@aol.com

Brad Bortner
U.S. Fish and Wildlife Service
911 NE 11th Ave.
Portland, OR 97232-4181
phone: 503-231-6164
fax: 503-231-2364
e-mail: brad_bortner@fws.gov

Frank Bowers
U.S. Fish and Wildlife Service
1875 Century Blvd., Suite 345
Atlanta, GA 30345
phone: 404-679-7188
fax: 404-679-7285
e-mail: frank_bowers@fws.gov

Dave Case
D.J. Case & Associates
607 Lincolnway West
Mishawaka, IN 46544
phone: 219-258-0100
fax: 219-258-0189
e-mail: dave@djcase.com

Dale Caswell
Canadian Wildlife Service
123 Main St. Suite 150
Winnepeg, Manitoba, CANADA R3C 4W2
phone: 204-983-5260
fax: 204-983-5248
e-mail: dale.caswell@ec.gc.ca

John Cornely
U.S. Fish and Wildlife Service
P.O. Box 25486, DFC
Denver, CO 80225
phone: 303-236-8155 (ext 259)
fax: 303-236-8680
e-mail: john_cornely@fws.gov

Gary Costanzo
Dept. of Game and Inland Fisheries
5806 Mooretown Road
Williamsburg, VA 23188
phone: 757-253-4180
fax: 757-253-4182
e-mail: gcostanzo@dgif.state.va.us

Jim Dubovsky
U.S. Fish & Wildlife Service
P.O. Box 25486 DFC
Denver, CO 80225-0486
phone: 303-236-8155 (ext 238)
fax: 303-236-8680
e-mail: james_dubovsky@fws.gov

Ken Gamble
U.S. Fish and Wildlife Service
608 Cherry Street, Room 119
Columbia, MO 65201
phone: 573-876-1915
fax: 573-876-1917
e-mail: ken_gamble@fws.gov

Jim Gammonley
Division of Wildlife
317 West Prospect
Fort Collins, CO 80526
phone: 970-472-4379
fax: 970-472-4457
e-mail: jim.gammonley@state.co.us

Pam Garrettson
U.S. Fish & Wildlife service
11500 American Holly Drive
Laurel, MD 20708-4016
phone: 301-497-5865
fax: 301-497-5871
e-mail: pam_garrettson@fws.gov

George Haas
U.S. Fish and Wildlife Service
300 Westgate Center Drive
Hadley, MA 01035-9589
phone: 413-253-8576
fax: 413-253-8480
e-mail: george_haas@fws.gov

Jeff Haskins
U.S. Fish and Wildlife Service
P.O. Box 1306
Albuquerque, NM 87103
phone: 505-248-6827 (ext 30)
fax: 505-248-7885
e-mail: jeff_haskins@fws.gov

Dale Humburg
Dept. of Conservation
Fish & Wildlife Research Center
1110 South College Ave.
Columbia, MO 65201
phone: 573-882-9880 (ext 3246)
fax: 573-882-4517
e-mail: humbud@mail.conservation.state.mo.us

Fred Johnson
U.S. Fish & Wildlife Service
7920 NW 71st Street
Gainesville, FL 32653
phone: 352-378-8181 (ext 372)
fax: 352-378-4956
e-mail: fred_a_johnson@fws.gov

Mike Johnson
Game and Fish Department
100 North Bismarck Expressway
Bismarck, ND 58501-5095
phone: 701-328-6319
fax: 701-328-6352
e-mail: mjohnson@state.nd.us

Jim Kelley
U.S. Fish and Wildlife Service
Division of Migratory Bird Management
BH Whipple Federal Building, 1 Federal Drive
Fort Snelling, MN 55111-4056
phone: 612-713-5409
fax: 612-713-5286
e-mail: james_r_kelley@fws.gov

Bill Kendall
U.S.G.S. Patuxent Wildlife Research Center
11510 American Holly Drive
Laurel, MD 20708-4017
phone: 301-497-5868
fax: 301-497-5666
e-mail: william_kendall@usgs.gov

Don Kraege
Dept. of Fish & Wildlife
600 Capital Way North
Olympia. WA 98501-1091
phone: 360-902-2509
fax: 360-902-2162
e-mail: kraegdkk@dfw.wa.gov

Bob Leedy
U.S. Fish and Wildlife Service
1011 East Tudor Road
Anchorage, AK 99503-6119
phone: 907-786-3446
fax: 907-786-3641
e-mail: robert_leedy@fws.gov

Mary Moore
U.S. Fish & Wildlife Service
206 Concord Drive
Watkinsville, GA 30677
phone: 706-769-2359
fax: 706-769-2359
e-mail: mary_moore@fws.gov

Jim Nichols
Patuxent Wildlife Research Center
11510 American Holly Drive
Laurel, MD 20708-4017
phone: 301-497-5660
fax: 301-497-5666
e-mail: jim_nichols@usgs.gov

Mark Otto
U.S. Fish & Wildlife Service
11500 American Holly Drive
Laurel, MD 20708-4016
phone: 301-497-5872
fax: 301-497-5871
e-mail: mark_otto@fws.gov

Paul Padding
U.S. Fish & Wildlife Service
10815 Loblolly Pine Drive
Laurel, MD 20708-4028
phone: 301-497-5980
fax: 301-497-5981
e-mail: paul_padding@fws.gov

Michael C. Runge
Patuxent Wildlife Research Center
11510 American Holly Drive
Laurel, MD 20708-4017
phone: 301-497-5748
fax: 301-497-5666
e-mail: michael_runge@usgs.gov

Jerry Serie
U.S. Fish & Wildlife Service
12100 Beech Forest Road
Laurel, MD 20708-4038
phone: 301-497-5851
fax: 301-497-5885
e-mail: jerry_serie@fws.gov

Dave Sharp
U.S. Fish and Wildlife Service
P.O. Box 25486, DFC
Denver, CO 80225-0486
phone: 303-275-2385
fax: 303-275-2384
e-mail: dave_sharp@fws.gov

Sue Sheaffer
Coop. Fish & Wildl. Research Unit
Fernow Hall, Cornell University
Ithaca, NY 14853
phone: 607-255-2837
fax: 607-255-1895
e-mail: ses11@cornell.edu

Graham Smith
U.S. Fish & Wildlife Service
11500 American Holly Drive
Laurel, MD 20708-4016
phone: 301-497-5860
fax: 301-497-5871
e-mail: graham_smith@fws.gov

Bryan Swift
Dept.of Environmental Conservation
108 Game Farm Road, Building 9
Delmar, NY 12054-9767
phone: 518-478-3022
fax: 518-478-3004
e-mail: bl.swift@gw.dec.state.ny.us

Bob Trost
U.S. Fish and Wildlife Service
911 NE 11th Ave.
Portland, OR 97232-4181
phone: 503-231-6162
fax: 503-231-6228
e-mail: robert_trost@fws.gov

Khristi Wilkins
U.S. Fish & Wildlife Service
11500 American Holly Drive
Laurel, MD 20708-4016
phone: 301-497-5557
fax: 301-497-5971
e-mail: khristi_a_wilkins@fws.gov

Dan Yparraguirre
Dept. of Fish & Game
1416 Ninth Street
Sacramento, CA 94244
phone: 916-653-8709
fax: 916-653-1019
e-mail: dyparrag@hq.dfg.ca.gov

APPENDIX B: Mallard Population Models

State and random variable definitions:

MBPOP   /* state variable index - midcontinent population */
PONDS   /* state variable index - Canadian ponds */
EBPOP   /* state variable index - eastern population */
RRES   /* random variable index - recruitment residuals for eastern population */
SSFVAR   /* random variable index - female summer survival - eastern population */
SSFRES   /* random variable index - residuals for female summer survival - eastern population */
PPT   /* random variable index - Canadian Prairie precipitation */
PROP   /* random variable index - proportion of midcontinent population in Lake States */
MRATE   /* random variable index - harvest rate - midcontinent adult males */
ERATE/* random variable index - harvest rate - eastern adult males */
outcome[ ]   /* outcome of random variable */
cur_state[ ] /* current value of state variable */
nxt_state[ ] /* value of state variable in next time step */

Eastern mallard parameters:

wtr1b1s1   /* weight for model r1b1s1 - neg. exp. reproduction, log. BBS, constant survival */
wtr1b1s2   /* weight for model r1b1s2 - neg. exp. reprod., log. BBS, density-dependent survival */
wtr1b2s1   /* weight for model r1b2s1 - neg. exp. reprod., exp. BBS, constant survival */
wtr1b2s2   /* weight for model r1b2s2 - neg. exp. reprod., exp. BBS, density-dependent survival */
wtr2b1s1   /* weight for model r2b1s1 - logistic reprod., log. BBS, constant survival */
wtr2b1s2   /* weight for model r2b1s2 - logistic reprod., log. BBS, density-dependent survival */
wtr2b2s1   /* weight for model r2b2s1 - logistic reprod., exp. BBS, constant survival */
wtr2b2s2   /* weight for model r2b2s2 - logistic reprod., exp. BBS, density-dependent survival */
nxr1b1s1   /* model-specific prediction of population size in next time step */
nxr1b1s2   /* model-specific prediction of population size in next time step */
nxr1b2s1   /* model-specific prediction of population size in next time step */
nxr1b2s2   /* model-specific prediction of population size in next time step */
nxr2b1s1   /* model-specific prediction of population size in next time step */
nxr2b1s2   /* model-specific prediction of population size in next time step */
nxr2b2s1   /* model-specific prediction of population size in next time step */
nxr2b2s2   /* model-specific prediction of population size in next time step */
Ne   /* breeding population size */
bbsb1   /* BBS index - logarithmic model */
bbsb2   /* BBS index - exponential[max] model */
ar1b1   /* male age ratio - neg. exp. reproduction - log. BBS */
ar1b2   /* male age ratio - neg. exp. reproduction - exponential[max] BBS */
ar2b1   /* male age ratio - logistic reproduction - log. BBS */
ar2b2   /* male age ratio - logistic reproduction - exponential[max] BBS */
hafe   /* harvest rate - adult females */
hame   /* harvest rate - adult males */
hyfe   /* harvest rate - young females */
hyme   /* harvest rate - young males */
kafe   /* kill rate - adult females */
kame   /* kill rate - adult males */
kyfe   /* kill rate - young females */
kyme   /* kill rate - young males */

```
dafe=1.19        /* differential vulnerability - adult females */
dyme=1.47        /* differential vulnerability - young males */
dyfe=1.62        /* differential vulnerability - yong females */
ce=0.2           /* crippling loss rate */
swe=0.90         /* winter survival */
ssme=0.81        /* summer survival - males */
ssfvar           /* summer survival - females - random variation */
ssfmb1 /* summer survival - females - density dependent survival - log. BBS */
ssfmb2 /* summer survival - females - density dependent survival - exponential[max] BBS */
sexe=0.55        /* proportion males in May */
```

Eastern mallard dynamics:

```
hame  =  outcome[ERATE];
hafe  =  min(1.0, hame*dafe);
hyme  =  min(1.0, hame*dyme);
hyfe  =  min(1.0, hame*dyfe);
kafe  =  min(1.0, hafe/(1-ce) );
kame  =  min(1.0, hame/(1-ce) );
kyfe  =  min(1.0, hyfe/(1-ce) );
kyme  =  min(1.0, hyme/(1-ce) );
bbsb1 = 0.6185*exp(1.3534*cur_state[EBPOP]/1000000);
bbsb2 = 11292.7921*(1-exp(-0.0002*cur_state[EBPOP]/1000000));
ar1b1 = max(0.0, (1.7330*exp(-0.2036*bbsb1))+outcome[RRES]);
ar1b2 = max(0.0, (1.7330*exp(-0.2036*bbsb2))+outcome[RRES]);
ar2b1 = max(0.0, (1.5027/(1+exp(-(bbsb1-2.8608)/-0.6490)))+outcome[RRES]);
ar2b2 = max(0.0, (1.5027/(1+exp(-(bbsb2-2.8608)/-0.6490)))+outcome[RRES]);
ssfvar = outcome[SSFVAR];
ssfmb1 = exp(1.6746-0.5422*bbsb1+outcome[SSFRES])/(1+exp(1.6746-0.5422*bbsb1+outcome[SSFRES]));
ssfmb2 = exp(1.6746-0.5422*bbsb2+outcome[SSFRES])/(1+exp(1.6746-0.5422*bbsb2+outcome[SSFRES]));
Ne = cur_state[EBPOP];
nxr1b1s1=max(0.0, Ne*((1-sexe)*ssfvar*(1-kafe)*swe + sexe*ssme*(1-kame)*swe +
      (sexe)*ssme*ar1b1*(1-kyfe)*swe + (sexe)*ssme*ar1b1*(1-kyme)*swe));
nxr1b1s2=max(0.0, Ne*((1-sexe)*ssfmb1*(1-kafe)*swe + sexe*ssme*(1-kame)*swe +
      (sexe)*ssme*ar1b1*(1-kyfe)*swe + (sexe)*ssme*ar1b1*(1-kyme)*swe));
nxr1b2s1=max(0.0, Ne*((1-sexe)*ssfvar*(1-kafe)*swe + sexe*ssme*(1-kame)*swe +
      (sexe)*ssme*ar1b2*(1-kyfe)*swe + (sexe)*ssme*ar1b2*(1-kyme)*swe));
nxr1b2s2=max(0.0, Ne*((1-sexe)*ssfmb2*(1-kafe)*swe + sexe*ssme*(1-kame)*swe +
      (sexe)*ssme*ar1b2*(1-kyfe)*swe + (sexe)*ssme*ar1b2*(1-kyme)*swe));
nxr2b1s1=max(0.0, Ne*((1-sexe)*ssfvar*(1-kafe)*swe + sexe*ssme*(1-kame)*swe +
      (sexe)*ssme*ar2b1*(1-kyfe)*swe + (sexe)*ssme*ar2b1*(1-kyme)*swe));
nxr2b1s2=max(0.0, Ne*((1-sexe)*ssfmb1*(1-kafe)*swe + sexe*ssme*(1-kame)*swe +
      (sexe)*ssme*ar2b1*(1-kyfe)*swe + (sexe)*ssme*ar2b1*(1-kyme)*swe));
nxr2b2s1=max(0.0, Ne*((1-sexe)*ssfvar*(1-kafe)*swe + sexe*ssme*(1-kame)*swe +
      (sexe)*ssme*ar2b2*(1-kyfe)*swe + (sexe)*ssme*ar2b2*(1-kyme)*swe));
nxr2b2s2=max(0.0, Ne*((1-sexe)*ssfmb2*(1-kafe)*swe + sexe*ssme*(1-kame)*swe +
      (sexe)*ssme*ar2b2*(1-kyfe)*swe + (sexe)*ssme*ar2b2*(1-kyme)*swe));
nxt_state[EBPOP] =
      max(0.0,nxr1b1s1*wtr1b1s1+nxr1b1s2*wtr1b1s2+nxr1b2s1*wtr1b2s1+nxr1b2s2*wtr1b2s2+
      nxr2b1s1*wtr2b1s1+nxr2b1s2*wtr2b1s2+nxr2b2s1*wtr2b2s1+nxr2b2s2*wtr2b2s2);
```

Midcontinent mallard parameters:

```
wt1              /* model 1 weight - compensatory mortality, strong density-dependent reproduction (ScRs) */
```

```
wt2          /* model 2 weight - compensatory mortality, weak density-dependent reprod. (ScRw) */
wt3          /* model 3 weight - additive mortality, strong density-dependent reprod. (SaRs) */
wt4          /* model 4 weight - additive mortality - weak density-dependent reprod. (SaRw) */
nxt1         /* model-specific prediction of population size in next time step */
nxt2         /* model-specific prediction of population size in next time step */
nxt3         /* model-specific prediction of population size in next time step */
nxt4         /* model-specific prediction of population size in next time step */
Nm           /* breeding population size */
P            /* May ponds in Prairie Canada */
Ai           /* fall age ratio - females - weakly density-dependent reproduction */
Ad           /* fall age ratio - females - strongly density-dependent reproduction */
Hafm         /* harvest rate - adult females */
Hamm         /* harvest rate - adult males */
Hyfm         /* harvest rate - young females */
Hymm         /* harvest rate - young males */
Kafm         /* kill rate - adult females */
Kamm         /* kill rate - adult males */
Kyfm         /* kill rate - young females */
Kymm         /* kill rate - young males */
shafim       /* hunt season survival - adult females - additive mortality */
shafdm /* hunt season survival - adult females - compensatory mortality */
shamim       /* hunt season survival - adult males - additive mortality */
shamdm       /* hunt season survival - adult males - compensatory mortality */
shyfim       /* hunt season survival - young females - additive mortality */
shyfdm /* hunt season survival - young females - compensatory mortality */
shymim       /* hunt season survival - young males - additive mortality */
shymdm       /* hunt season survival - young males - compensatory mortality */
dafm=0.748   /* differential vulnerability - adult females */
dymm=1.361   /* differential vulnerability - young males */
dyfm=1.188   /* differential vulnerability - young females */
cm=0.2 /* crippling loss rate */
s0m=0.81     /* survival in absence of hunting - male */
s0f=0.64     /* survival in absence of hunting - female */
swm=0.90     /* winter survival */
ssmm=0.90    /* summer survival - males */
ssfm=0.71    /* summer survival - females */
ctf=0.36     /* compensatory threshold - females */
ctm=0.19     /* compensatory threshold - males */
sexm=0.55    /* proportion of males in May */
```

Midcontinent mallard dynamics:

```
Nm = cur_state[MBPOP];
P = cur_state[PONDS];
Hamm = outcome[MRATE];
Hafm  =  min(1.0, Hamm*dafm);
Hymm  =  min(1.0, Hamm*dymm);
Hyfm  =  min(1.0, Hamm*dyfm);
Kafm  =  min(1.0, Hafm/(1-cm) );
Kamm  =  min(1.0, Hamm/(1-cm) );
Kyfm  =  min(1.0, Hyfm/(1-cm) );
Kymm  =  min(1.0, Hymm/(1-cm) );
Ai = max(0.0, 0.8249-(0.0547*((1-outcome[PROP])*Nm/1000000.0))+(0.1130*(P/1000000.0)));
Ad = max(0.0, 1.1081-(0.1128*((1-outcome[PROP])*Nm/1000000.0))+(0.1460*(P/1000000.0)));
```

```
shafim=(1-Kafm); shamim=(1-Kamm); shyfim=(1-Kyfm); shymim=(1-Kymm);
if (Kafm>ctf) shafdm=(1-Kafm)/s0f; else shafdm=1.0;
if (Kamm>ctm) shamdm=(1-Kamm)/s0m; else shamdm=1.0;
if (Kyfm>ctf) shyfdm=(1-Kyfm)/s0f; else shyfdm=1.0;
if (Kymm>ctm) shymdm=(1-Kymm)/s0m; else shymdm=1.0;
nxt_state[PONDS] = max(1.0, -3835087.53+0.45*P+13695.47*outcome[PPT]) ;
nxt1=Nm*((1.-sexm)*ssfm*(shafdm+Ad*(shyfdm+shymdm)) + sexm*ssmm*shamdm)*swm;
nxt2=Nm*((1.-sexm)*ssfm*(shafdm+Ai*(shyfdm+shymdm)) + sexm*ssmm*shamdm)*swm;
nxt3=Nm*((1.-sexm)*ssfm*(shafim+Ad*(shyfim+shymim)) + sexm*ssmm*shamim)*swm;
nxt4=Nm*((1.-sexm)*ssfm*(shafim+Ai*(shyfim+shymim)) + sexm*ssmm*shamim)*swm;
nxt_state[MBPOP] = max(0.0, wt1*nxt1+wt2*nxt2+wt3*nxt3+wt4*nxt4);
```

APPENDIX C: Updating of Model Weights

Adaptive harvest management prescribes regulations for midcontinent mallards based on passive adaptive optimization using weighted models of population and harvest dynamics (Johnson et al. 1997). We update model weights (or probabilities) based on how predictions from each of the four population models compare to the observed breeding population in year $t+1$. This posterior updating of model probabilities is based on a version of Bayes Theorem:

$$p_{t+1}(model\ i\ |\ data) = \frac{p_t(model\ i)\ p_{t+1}(data\ |\ model\ i)}{\sum_j p_t(model\ j)\ p_{t+1}(data\ |\ model\ j)}, \tag{1}$$

where $p_t(model\ i)$ is the probability that *model i* is correct. We assume that some element of our model set is the "correct" model for the system, and remains the correct model throughout. Equation (1), then, tracks the probability that each of the candidate models is the correct one through time. The state of the system in year $t+1$ consists of breeding population size (N_{t+1}) and number of ponds (P_{t+1}). Under our current approach, information on ponds in year $t+1$ is not informative with respect to updating model probabilities in year t, because all four candidate models predict the same number of ponds every year. We can rewrite the likelihood above as:

$$p_{t+1}(data\ |\ model\ i) = f\left(N_{t+1}^{data}\ |\ \hat{N}_{t+1}^{(i)}\right), \tag{2}$$

where N_{t+1}^{data} comes from the Breeding Waterfowl and Habitat Survey (May Survey), and $\hat{N}_{t+1}^{(i)}$ is the predicted size of the population based on *model i*.

A formal approach involves modeling the conditional likelihood in (2) as a normal distribution:

$$f\left(N_{t+1}^{data}\ |\ \hat{N}_{t+1}^{(i)}\right) \sim normal[E(N_{t+1}^{data}|\hat{N}_{t+1}^{(i)}),\ Var(N_{t+1}^{data}\ |\ \hat{N}_{t+1}^{(i)})]. \tag{3}$$

This form is intuitively appealing, because the value of the likelihood for the observed population size will depend on:

$$\frac{N_{t+1}^{data} - E(N_{t+1}^{data}|\hat{N}_{t+1}^{(i)})}{\sqrt{var(N_{t+1}^{data}|\hat{N}_{t+1}^{(i)})}},$$

which includes the difference between the observed population size and that predicted by *model i*, and the variance in the observed state of the system one would expect under *model I*.

Next, we must address the estimation of the mean and variance of $f(N_{t+1}^{data}|\hat{N}_{t+1}^{(i)})$. First,

$$\hat{N}_{t+1}^{(i)} = g^{(i)}\left(N_t^{data},\ P_t^{data},\ \{h_{as}\}_t\right), \tag{4}$$

where $g^{(i)}$ is a model-specific description of population dynamics and $\{h_{as}\}_t$ is the set of age- and sex-specific harvest rates in year t. All of the models we are considering are stochastic, allowing for partial controllability of the system (i.e., h_{as} is a random variable whose distribution is based on the regulatory package that is chosen in year t). In addition, N_t^{data} and P_t^{data} are subject to error, due to partial observability of the system (i.e., sampling variation in the May

Survey), but we assume they are unbiased estimators. Therefore $\hat{N}_{t+1}^{(i)}$ is subject to error in predicting the actual population size, N_{t+1}, under *model i*. Based on this we derive the mean and variance of interest using conditional arguments:

$$E[N_{t+1}^{data}|\hat{N}_{t+1}^{(i)}] = E_{N_{t+1}}[E(N_{t+1}^{data}|N_{t+1}, \hat{N}_{t+1}^{(i)})] = E(N_{t+1}|\hat{N}_{t+1}^{(i)}) = \hat{N}_{t+1}^{(i)} , \qquad (5)$$

$$Var[N_{t+1}^{data}|\hat{N}_{t+1}^{(i)}] = E_{N_{t+1}}[Var(N_{t+1}^{data}|N_{t+1}, \hat{N}_{t+1}^{(i)})] \\ + Var_{N_{t+1}}[E(N_{t+1}^{data}|N_{t+1}, \hat{N}_{t+1}^{(i)})] . \qquad (6)$$

We estimate the first term in equation (6) with the sampling variance from the May Survey in year $t+1$. The second term can be simplified to:

$$Var_{N_{t+1}}[E(N_{t+1}^{data} | N_{t+1}, \hat{N}_{t+1}^{(i)})] = Var [N_{t+1} | \hat{N}_{t+1}^{(i)}], \qquad (7)$$

Therefore (6) can be reexpressed as:

$$\hat{Var}[N_{t+1}^{data} | \hat{N}_{t+1}^{(i)}] = sampling\ variance + \hat{Var} [N_{t+1} | \hat{N}_{t+1}^{(i)}] , \qquad (8)$$

The variance in the second term of (8) is derived from the sources of uncertainty inherent in the function in (4): partial observability of the state of the system, and partial controllability of harvest, in year t.

We use parametric bootstrapping for approximating the likelihood in (2) without assuming a distributional form. It also precludes the need to derive an explicit estimate of the variance in (8). Instead we assume distributional forms for more basic quantities.

We simulate the transition from the state of the system in year t, to the state of the system in year $t+1$, under each model, described by g in (4). We acknowledge uncertainty about the values of N_t, P_t, and $\{h_{as}\}_t$, and to incorporate this uncertainty we use random values from the following assumed distributions in their place:

$$f(N_t^{boot}) \sim normal[N_t^{data}, Var(N_t^{data}|N_t)], \\ f(P_t^{boot}) \sim normal[P_t^{data}, Var(P_t^{data}|N_t)], \qquad (9) \\ f(h_{ast}^{boot}) \sim normal[\hat{h}_{ast}, Var(\hat{h}_t|h_{ast})].$$

Because we anticipate a sampling covariance between N_t^{data} and P_t^{data}, and do not currently have an estimate of its value, we make the conservative (i.e., largest $Var[N_{t+1}^{data}|\hat{N}_{t+1}^{(i)}]$ possible) assumption that the two are perfectly correlated. Practically speaking, this implies that the simulation of these two random variables will be based on the same draw from a standard normal distribution.

Because we update the model probabilities after direct recovery rates are available from the hunting season in year t, we use estimates and sampling variances of realized harvest rates (recovery rates, adjusted for reporting rate) in the updating process whenever possible. Because there is no sampling covariance between estimates of harvest rate for the four age-sex classes, we generate an independent normal random variate for each.

34

For each model, in each repetition of the simulation, the generated value of N_t is projected to the actual value of N_{t+1} ($N_{t+1}^{(i)boot}$). Finally, to represent partial observability in year $t+1$, we generate another random number from the following distribution:

$$N_{t+1}^{data}|N_{t+1}^{(i)boot} \sim normal[N_{t+1}^{(i)boot},(c.v.(N_{t+1}^{data})\cdot N_{t+1}^{(i)boot})^2]. \qquad (10)$$

We base the variance of the model-dependent distribution in (10) on the estimated coefficient of variation from the May Survey, instead of its variance, because experience has shown that the standard error is proportional to population size. This process produces an observed population size in year $t+1$ for each repetition of the simulation. By repeating the process a large number of times we produce an empirical distribution to compare against the realized N_{t+1}^{data} from the May Survey. We use 10,000 iterations and then use smoothing techniques to estimate a likelihood function. Finally, we determine the likelihood value for *model i* based on N_{t+1}^{data}, and incorporate it into equations (2) and (1).

APPENDIX D: Predicting Harvest Rates

This procedure involves: (1) linear models that predict total seasonal mallard harvest for varying regulations (daily bag limit and season length), while accounting for trends in numbers of successful duck hunters; and (2) use of these models to adjust historical estimates of mallard harvest rates to reflect differences in bag limit, season length and trends in hunter numbers. Using historical data from both the U.S. Waterfowl Mail Questionnaire and Parts Collection Surveys, and with the use of several key assumptions, the resulting models allowed us to predict total seasonal mallard harvest and associated predicted harvest rates for varying combinations of season length and daily bag limits.

Total seasonal mallard harvest is predicted using two separate models: the "harvest" model which predicts average daily mallard harvest per successful duck hunter for each day of the hunting season (Table D-1), and the "hunter" model which predicts the number of successful duck hunters (Table D-2). The "harvest" model uses as the dependent variable the square root of the average daily mallard harvest (per successful duck hunter). The independent variables include the consecutive day of the hunting season (splits were ignored), daily mallard bag limit, season length, and the interaction of bag limit and season length. Also included is an effect representing the opening day (of the first split), an effect representing a week (7 day) effect, and several other interaction terms. Seasonal mallard harvest per successful duck hunter is obtained by back-transforming the predicted values that resulted from the model, and summing the average daily harvest over the season length. The "hunter" model uses information on the numbers of successful duck hunters (based on duck stamp sales information) from 1981-95. Using daily bag limit and season length as independent variables, the number of successful duck hunters is predicted for each state.

Both the "harvest" and "hunter" models were developed for each of seven management areas: the Atlantic Flyway portion with compensatory days; the Atlantic Flyway portion without compensatory days; the Mississippi Flyway; the low plains portion of Central Flyway; the High Plains Mallard Management Unit in the Central Flyway; the Columbia Basin Mallard Management Unit in the Pacific Flyway; and the remainder of the Pacific Flyway excluding Alaska. The numbers of successful hunters predicted at the state level are summed to obtain a total number (H) for each management area. Likewise, the "harvest" model results in a seasonal mallard harvest per successful duck hunter (A) for each management area. Total seasonal mallard harvest (T) is formed by the product of H and A.

To compare total seasonal mallard harvest under different regulatory alternatives, ratios of T are formed for each management area and then combined into a weighted mean. *Under the key assumption that the ratio of harvest rates realized under two different regulatory alternatives is equal to the expected ratio of total harvest obtained under the same two alternatives*, the harvest rate experienced under the historic "liberal" package (1979-84) was adjusted by T to produce predicted harvest rates for the current regulatory alternatives.

The models developed here were not designed, nor are able, to predict mallard harvest rates directly. The procedure relies heavily on statistical and conceptual models that must meet certain assumptions. We have no way to verify these assumptions, nor can we gauge their effects should they not be met. The use of this procedure for predicting mallard harvest rates for regulations alternatives for which we have little or no experience warrants considerable caution.

Table D-1. Parameter estimates by management area for models of seasonal harvest per successful hunter.

Model effect[a]	AF- COMP.	AF-NOCOMP	MF	CF-lp	CF-HP	PF-CB	PF
INTERCEPT	0.378359	0.555790	0.485971	0.554667	0.593799	0.736258	0.543791
(SE)	(0.061477)	(0.134516)	(0.037175)	(0.041430)	(0.059649)	(0.154315)	(0.054712)
OPEN	0.194945	0.263793	0.175012	0.092507	0.113074	0.361696	0.322255
(SE)	(0.010586)	(0.018365)	(0.011258)	(0.015623)	(0.018530)	(0.040605)	(0.012730)
WEEK	0.024232	0.040392	-0.016479	-0.108472	-0.074895	-0.063422	-0.060477
(SE)	(0.006561)	(0.011436)	(0.006965)	(0.008860)	(0.009437)	(0.018220)	(0.006118)
WEEK2	-0.003586	-0.006823	0.000422	0.010472	0.006782	0.003573	0.004893
(SE)	(0.000796)	(0.001392)	(0.000847)	(0.001075)	(0.001150)	(0.002266)	(0.000746)
WK*SDAY	-0.001245	-0.001395	-0.000073	0.002578	0.001222	-0.000102	0.000116
(SE)	(0.000231)	(0.000407)	(0.000248)	(0.000260)	(0.000215)	(0.000289)	(0.000120)
WK2*SDAY	0.000163	0.000219	0.000052	-0.000271	-0.000109	0.000045	0.000007
(SE)	(0.000028)	(0.000050)	(0.000030)	(0.000032)	(0.000026)	(0.000037)	(0.000015)
SEASDAY	0.000419	-0.001034	-0.002559	-0.006322	-0.003174	-0.000615	-0.000909
(SE)	(0.000407)	(0.000712)	(0.000434)	(0.000464)	(0.000382)	(0.000476)	(0.000209)
MALBAG	-0.025557	-0.062755	0.026729	0.016049	-0.029753	-0.049532	-0.021774
(SE)	(0.019282)	(0.043020)	(0.015007)	(0.010766)	(0.013918)	(0.047903)	(0.017457)
SEASLEN	-0.004852	-0.008836	-0.004869	-0.001250	-0.003089	0.001562	-0.001931
(SE)	(0.001260)	(0.002750)	(0.000768)	(0.000833)	(0.000995)	(0.001682)	(0.000591)
BAG*SEAS	0.000926	0.002018	0.000332	-0.000033	0.000732	0.000024	0.000328
(SE)	(0.000393)	(0.000877)	(0.000310)	(0.000202)	(0.000216)	(0.000464)	(0.000184)

[a]Model Effect   Description

INTERCEPT	Intercept
OPEN	Opening Day of First Split (Y,N)
WEEK	Day of Week (1,2,3,4,5,6,7)
WEEK2	Week * Week (Quadratic Effect)
WK*SDAY	Week * Day of Season Interaction
WK2*SDAY	Week * Week * Day of Season Interaction
SEASDAY	Day of Season (Consecutive)
MALBAG	Daily Mallard Bag Limit
SEASLEN	Season Length
BAG*SEAS	Daily Mallard Bag Limit * Season Length Interaction

Table D-2. Parameter estimates by management area for models to predict hunter numbers.

Mgmt Area	Effect	State/Zone	Estimate	SE	Mgmt Area	Effect	State/Zone	Estimate	SE
AF-Comp.	Malbag		-229.854	320.613	CF - lp	Malbag		577.848	715.617
	Seaslen		119.595	28.473		Seaslen		317.973	100.931
	Intercepts:	CT	925.275	823.888		Intercepts:	KS	-6,006.131	3,108.375
		DE	376.732	829.784			NE	-4,997.796	3,114.451
		ME	3,581.062	825.956			ND	-3,930.604	3,021.002
		MD	10,712.000	809.333			OK	-8,010.002	3,208.936
		NJ	5,940.028	813.652			SD	-4,053.537	3,021.002
		NC	12,798.000	836.186			TX	33,480.000	3,021.002
		PA	17,683.000	822.566	CF - HP	Malbag		734.041	181.624
		VA	7,276.371	809.333		Seaslen		-1.332	16.318
		WV	-2,884.782	818.825		Intercepts:	CO	12,354.000	687.696
		MA_3	1,679.885	818.507			KS	-973.654	688.526
		MA_R	-336.288	843.081			MT	482.197	699.176
AF-No comp.	Malbag		71.885	188.301			NE	3,222.880	688.526
	Seaslen		62.574	18.776			NM	447.280	688.526
	Intercepts:	FL	9,709.872	530.458			ND	4,559.079	541.659
		GA	7,058.253	541.184			OK	-2,299.609	687.696
		RI	-1,515.873	543.352			SD	748.221	695.658
		SC	10,004.000	541.184			TX	2,817.864	695.658
		VT	679.453	541.184			WY	1,639.613	688.526
		NH_1	-1,536.280	541.184	PF - CB	Malbag		505.129	411.451
		NH_2	201.430	536.395		Seaslen		31.446	48.602
		NY_1	336.305	537.703		Intercepts:	OR	-3,910.659	2,311.323
		NY_2	-2,122.214	541.184			WA	5,433.261	2,334.479
		NY_5	7,070.786	541.184					
		NY_R	8,650.966	538.322					
		OH_1	-2,426.542	535.906					

Mgmt Area	Effect	State/Zone	Estimate	SE	Mgmt Area	Effect	State/Zone	Estimate	SE
MF	Malbag		-4,523.798	1,231.622	PF	Malbag		790.844	284.473
	Seaslen		897.413	120.583		Seaslen		59.303	31.696
	Intercepts:	AL	-15,044.000	2,361.763		Intercepts:	AZ	-3,958.814	1,402.487
		AR	5,599.384	2,361.763			CO	-4,832.461	1,400.722
		IL	7,438.650	2,361.763			ID	6,285.454	1,384.878
		IN	-13,932.000	2,361.763			MT	-887.114	1,458.939
		IA	-1,346.879	2,337.443			NV	-2,483.897	1,369.116
		KY	-15,477.000	2,394.393			NM	-7,588.133	1,395.432
		LA	41,690.000	2,543.303			OR	11,687.000	1,397.194
		MI	10,232.000	2,361.763			UT	6,803.640	1,415.495
		MN	61,174.000	2,635.798			WY	9,398.653	1,402.487
		MS	-9,207.288	2,285.436			CA_1	-3,696.948	1,385.102
		MO	-2,225.616	2,361.763			CA_2	-5,421.502	1,427.980
		TN	-6,958.016	2,361.763			CA_3	3,580.319	1,385.102
		WI	27,254.000	2,361.763			CA_4	-6,475.400	1,378.069
		OH_R	-9,163.989	2,635.798			CA_5	29,744.000	1,385.102

APPENDIX E: Estimating the Mallard Harvest Rate for the 2000-01 Season

We estimated the overall harvest rate of adult male mallards in the midcontinent region using harvest-rate estimates for reference areas 2, 4 and 5 (Anderson and Henny 1972) that were derived from reward banding. Harvest rates in the unsampled banding reference areas (1, 3, 6-7 and 12-14) were treated as missing, and conventional data augmentation (or multiple imputation) techniques were employed (Schafer 1997).

The model under which estimates were produced assumes that the vector of harvest rates for the ten reference areas is a multivariate normal random variable with some unknown mean vector and variance-covariance matrix. The variance-covariance matrix describes the correlations between harvest rate among the reference areas. Nominally, the harvest rate for a given reference area is correlated with the harvest rate in the other reference areas, and it is this aspect which facilitates estimation of "unobserved" harvest rates from those which are estimated from data. The mean vector and variance-covariance matrix in the model were estimated from 36 years of historic data.

Estimates and their variances were computed for each of the seven unsampled reference areas. These predictions were then weighted by the proportion of the midcontinent mallard population in each area during spring 2000 to construct an estimate of the overall harvest rate. The estimated harvest rate of adult-male mallards in the midcontinent region during the 2000-01 hunting season was 0.129 (SE = 0.011), which is well within the 90 percent confidence interval for harvest rate under the liberal regulatory alternative. The estimated harvest rates from the 1998-99 and 1999-2000 hunting seasons were 0.108 (SE = 0.013) and 0.098 (SE = 0.008), respectively.

Appendix F: Past Regulations and Harvest Strategies

Table F-1. Regulatory alternatives for the 1995 and 1996 duck-hunting seasons.

Regulation	Flyway			
	Atlantic	Mississippi	Central[a]	Pacific[b]
Shooting hours	one-half hour before sunrise to sunset for all Flyways			
Framework dates	Oct 1 - Jan 20	Saturday closest to October 1 and Sunday closest to January 20		
Season length (days)				
Restrictive	30	30	39	59
Moderate	40	40	51	79
Liberal	50	50	60	93
Bag limit (total / mallard / female mallard)				
Restrictive	3 / 3 / 1	3 / 2 / 1	3 / 3 / 1	4 / 3 / 1
Moderate	4 / 4 / 1	4 / 3 / 1	4 / 4 / 1	5 / 4 / 1
Liberal	5 / 5 / 1	5 / 4 / 1	5 / 5 / 1	6-7[c] / 6-7[c] / 1

[a] The High Plains Mallard Management Unit was allowed 12, 16, and 23 extra days under the restrictive, moderate, and liberal alternatives, respectively.

[b] The Columbia Basin Mallard Management Unit was allowed seven extra days under all three alternatives.

[c] The limits were 6 in 1995 and 7 in 1996.

Table F-2. Optimal regulatory choices[a] for midcontinent mallards during the 1995 hunting season. This strategy is based on the regulatory alternatives for 1995, equal weights for four alternative models of population dynamics, and the dual objectives of maximizing long-term cumulative harvest and achieving a population goal of 8.7 million.

Mallards[c]	Ponds[b]									
	1.5	2.0	2.5	3.0	3.5	4.0	4.5	5.0	5.5	6.0
4.5	M	M	M	L	L	L	L	L	L	L
5.0	L	L	L	L	L	L	L	L	L	L
5.5	L	L	L	L	L	L	L	L	L	L
6.0	L	L	L	L	L	L	L	L	L	L
6.5	L	L	L	L	L	L	L	L	L	L
7.0	L	L	L	L	L	L	L	L	L	L
7.5	L	L	L	L	L	L	L	L	L	L
8.0	L	L	L	L	L	L	L	L	L	L
8.5	L	L	L	L	L	L	L	L	L	L
9.0	L	L	L	L	L	L	L	L	L	L
9.5	L	L	L	L	L	L	L	L	L	L
10.0	L	L	L	L	L	L	L	L	L	L
10.5	L	L	L	L	L	L	L	L	L	L
11.0	L	L	L	L	L	L	L	L	L	L

[a] R = restrictive, M = moderate, and L = liberal.
[b] Estimated number of ponds in Prairie Canada in May, in millions.
[c] Estimated number of midcontinent mallards during May, in millions.

Table F-3. Optimal regulatory choices[a] for midcontinent mallards during the 1996 hunting season. This strategy is based on the regulatory alternatives and model weights for 1996, and the dual objectives of maximizing long-term cumulative harvest and achieving a population goal of 8.7 million.

Mallards[c]	Ponds[b]									
	1.5	2.0	2.5	3.0	3.5	4.0	4.5	5.0	5.5	6.0
4.5										
5.0								R	R	R
5.5					R	R	R	R	M	M
6.0	R	R	R	R	R	R	M	M	L	L
6.5	R	R	R	M	M	M	L	L	L	L
7.0	M	M	M	L	L	L	L	L	L	L
7.5	M	L	L	L	L	L	L	L	L	L
8.0	L	L	L	L	L	L	L	L	L	L
8.5	L	L	L	L	L	L	L	L	L	L
9.0	L	L	L	L	L	L	L	L	L	L
9.5	L	L	L	L	L	L	L	L	L	L
10.0	L	L	L	L	L	L	L	L	L	L
10.5	L	L	L	L	L	L	L	L	L	L
11.0	L	L	L	L	L	L	L	L	L	L

[a] R = restrictive, M = moderate, and L = liberal.
[b] Estimated number of ponds in Prairie Canada in May, in millions.
[c] Estimated number of midcontinent mallards during May, in millions.

Table F-4. Optimal regulatory choices[a] for midcontinent mallards during the 1997 hunting season. This strategy is based on regulatory alternatives and model weights for 1997, and on the dual objectives of maximizing long-term cumulative harvest and achieving a population goal of 8.7 million.

Mallards[c]	Ponds[b]									
	1.5	2.0	2.5	3.0	3.5	4.0	4.5	5.0	5.5	6.0
4.5										
5.0										
5.5								VR	VR	VR
6.0			VR	VR	VR	VR	VR	R	R	R
6.5	VR	VR	VR	VR	R	R	R	M	M	M
7.0	R	R	R	R	R	M	M	M	L	L
7.5	R	R	M	M	M	M	L	L	L	L
8.0	M	M	M	M	L	L	L	L	L	L
8.5	M	M	L	L	L	L	L	L	L	L
9.0	L	L	L	L	L	L	L	L	L	L
9.5	L	L	L	L	L	L	L	L	L	L
10.0	L	L	L	L	L	L	L	L	L	L
10.5	L	L	L	L	L	L	L	L	L	L
11.0	L	L	L	L	L	L	L	L	L	L

[a] VR = very restrictive, R = restrictive, M = moderate, and L = liberal.
[b] Estimated number of ponds in Prairie Canada in May, in millions.
[c] Estimated number of mid-continent mallards during May, in millions.

Table F-5. Optimal regulatory choices[a] for midcontinent mallards during the 1998 hunting season. This strategy is based on regulatory alternatives and model weights for 1998, and on the dual objectives of maximizing long-term cumulative harvest and achieving a population goal of 8.7 million.

Mallards[c]	Ponds[b]									
	1.5	2.0	2.5	3.0	3.5	4.0	4.5	5.0	5.5	6.0
4.5										
5.0										VR
5.5							VR	VR	VR	R
6.0		VR	VR	VR	VR	VR	R	R	R	M
6.5	VR	VR	VR	R	R	R	M	M	M	L
7.0	R	R	R	R	M	M	M	L	L	L
7.5	R	M	M	M	M	L	L	L	L	L
8.0	M	M	M	L	L	L	L	L	L	L
8.5	M	L	L	L	L	L	L	L	L	L
9.0	L	L	L	L	L	L	L	L	L	L
9.5	L	L	L	L	L	L	L	L	L	L
10.0	L	L	L	L	L	L	L	L	L	L
10.5	L	L	L	L	L	L	L	L	L	L
11.0	L	L	L	L	L	L	L	L	L	L

[a] VR = very restrictive, R = restrictive, M = moderate, and L = liberal.
[b] Estimated number of ponds in Prairie Canada in May, in millions.
[c] Estimated number of mid-continent mallards during May, in millions.

Table F-6. Optimal regulatory choices[a] for midcontinent mallards during the 1999 hunting season. This strategy is based on regulatory alternatives and model weights for 1999, and on the dual objectives of maximizing long-term cumulative harvest and achieving a population goal of 8.7 million.

Mallards[c]	Ponds[b]									
	1.5	2.0	2.5	3.0	3.5	4.0	4.5	5.0	5.5	6.0
<5.0										
5.0										VR
5.5							VR	VR	VR	R
6.0		VR	VR	VR	VR	VR	R	R	R	M
6.5	VR	VR	VR	R	R	R	M	M	M	L
7.0	R	R	R	R	M	M	M	L	L	L
7.5	R	M	M	M	M	L	L	L	L	L
8.0	M	M	M	L	L	L	L	L	L	L
8.5	M	L	L	L	L	L	L	L	L	L
9.0	L	L	L	L	L	L	L	L	L	L
9.5	L	L	L	L	L	L	L	L	L	L
10.0	L	L	L	L	L	L	L	L	L	L
10.5	L	L	L	L	L	L	L	L	L	L
11.0	L	L	L	L	L	L	L	L	L	L

[a] VR = very restrictive, R = restrictive, M = moderate, and L = liberal.
[b] Estimated number of ponds in Prairie Canada in May, in millions.
[c] Estimated number of midcontinent mallards during May, in millions.

Table F-7. Optimal regulatory choices[a] in the three western Flyways during the 2000 hunting season. This strategy is based on regulatory alternatives and model weights for 2000, and on the dual objectives of maximizing long-term cumulative harvest and achieving a population goal of 8.7 million midcontinent mallards.

Mallards[c]	Ponds[b]									
	1.5	2.0	2.5	3.0	3.5	4.0	4.5	5.0	5.5	6.0
<4.5										
4.5										VR
5.0						VR	VR	VR	R	R
5.5	VR	VR	VR	VR	VR	R	R	R	M	M
6.0	VR	R	R	R	R	M	M	M	L	L
6.5	R	R	M	M	M	M	L	L	L	L
7.0	M	M	M	M	L	L	L	L	L	L
7.5	M	M	L	L	L	L	L	L	L	L
8.0	L	L	L	L	L	L	L	L	L	L
8.5	L	L	L	L	L	L	L	L	L	L
9.0	L	L	L	L	L	L	L	L	L	L
9.5	L	L	L	L	L	L	L	L	L	L
10.0	L	L	L	L	L	L	L	L	L	L
10.5	L	L	L	L	L	L	L	L	L	L
11.0	L	L	L	L	L	L	L	L	L	L

[a] VR = very restrictive, R = restrictive, M = moderate, and L = liberal.
[b] Estimated number of ponds in Prairie Canada in May, in millions.
[c] Estimated number of midcontinent mallards during May, in millions.